Foreword by Dr. Temple Grandin

Recognizing

When It Has Been
Hidden Well

Autism in
Women & Girls

Wendela Whitcomb Marsh MA, BCBA, RSD

RECOGNIZING AUTISM IN WOMEN & GIRLS:
When It Has Been Hidden Well

All marketing and publishing rights guaranteed to and reserved by:

FUTURE HORIZONS

(817) 277-0727
(817) 277-2270 (fax)
E-mail: info@fhautism.com
www.fhautism.com

ISBN: 9781949177848

This book is for

Cat David Robinson Marsh

Siobhan Eleanor Wise Marsh

Noel Maebh Whitcomb Marsh

and forever in our hearts

David Scott Marsh

Acknowledgments

There are so many people to recognize for their contributions to this book.

I am grateful for the unconditional love of my parents, Drs. David and Susanne Whitcomb, and my beloved, David Scott Marsh. They recognized in me strengths I did not always see in myself, and their influence lives on.

My three brilliant children, Cat David Robinson Marsh, Siobhan Eleanor Wise Marsh, and Noel Maebh Whitcomb Marsh. I am daily inspired by your courage in a world that can be overwhelming, your ingenuity to find creative ways to overcome barriers, your commitment to the world, to each other, and to who you are. Also, you are excellent company during a global pandemic, or any time.

My talented siblings, authors all: Jonathan David Whitcomb, Cynthia Susanne Whitcomb, Laura Louise Whitcomb. You make me want to write more, to keep up with you.

The women in our Writers Support Group and the Chez Authors Who Lunch: Susan Fletcher, Pamela Smith Hill, Linda Leslie, Kristi Negri, Cherie Walters, Cynthia Whitcomb, Laura Whitcomb. Your encouragement means so much!

Diane Hagood, for your friendship, your insights, and for helping me recognize what's important in life.

Early readers and editors, Siobhan Marsh and Cynthia Whitcomb, for catching many errors and shining a light on ways to make this a better book.

Special recognition for the autistic women and trans and nonbinary individuals who shared their stories for *In Her Own Words* to help educate others: Jessica Dawn, Reese Dawson, Shanda K, Kara, Molly, Jansen Niccals, Denise S, Nakeba Todd. Contributions have been edited for brevity and clarity, but the stories are all your own. Your generosity in sharing your experiences will help open eyes and doors for many more.

Autistic women and trans folk who have inspired me: authors Karletta Abianac, Judy Endow, Temple Grandin, Sarah Hendrickx, Wenn Lawson, Anita Lesko, Jennifer O'Toole, Yenn Purkis, Rudy Simone, Maxfield Sparrow, Liane Holliday Wiley, and many, many more.

The extensive research and writings of Dr. Tony Attwood, especially his dedication to the issue of autism in girls, has provided a guiding light for me and for all of us who follow.

I am grateful beyond words to be part of the Future Horizons, Inc. family. Thank you all, especially president Jennifer Gilpin Yacio and editorial director Rose Heredia-Bechtel.

Finally, to all of the people I have worked with and diagnosed over the years, thank you for recognizing that special something within you that resonated with autism and for reaching out in search of answers. I have learned so much from you, and it has been a joy to share a small part of your journey!

TABLE OF CONTENTS

There is so much in this book that I relate to as a woman with autism. As I read these fictional examples of autistic girls, I can really identify with them. Even as an adult, I have the tendency to lecture and give people all the latest scientific news on things like COVID-19 or dog behavior. I just love talking about stuff that I find absolutely fascinating, such as preventing power plants from freezing.

One of the things I cannot do so well is quick back-and-forth chitchat. I get in a conversation where people are chitchatting back and forth and it goes so fast, I can't follow it.

It also gives me a problem with interrupting. People say that I interrupt, and I do interrupt, but it is because I cannot get the timing right. It has to do with processor speed of the brain, so for the kind of chitchat conversations where people are just loving it, I don't have the processor speed to take part.

When I was at the University of Illinois, I was socially awkward, and some people thought I was stuck-up because I didn't say hi to people in the hallway. *But that is something I learned how to do.* Another one of the examples in the book discussed laughing about unrelated things. This happens to me. I might be talking about one movie and, as you talk about another movie, then I just start laughing about it, or if we are out driving and I see a certain kind of car out on the highway that reminds me of something, then I just have to tell everybody even though it's not related to the conversation. I'm more interested in intellectual stuff, stuff I do.

A lot of people are social-emotional. Social-emotional makes the world go around. But what makes the world go around for me is doing or talking about intellectual interesting things. A brain can be more cognitive-intellectual, or it can be more social-emotional. Now, a certain amount of this is just normal variation—but we need the people in the world who are interested in things. We need people who are interested in keeping the power systems on to keep the world working.

INTRODUCTION

Opening the Door for Autistic Girls & Women

"When doctors, parents, teachers, therapists, even television describe typical spectrum kids, without meaning to, they're describing typically male spectrum traits—patterns first noticed by observing boys. Only boys. And we aren't boys. So they miss and mislabel us."

— *Jennifer O'Toole, autistic author*

The Myth

Autism Spectrum Disorder (ASD) has historically been regarded as a condition that affects males significantly more often than females. In 2016 the Center for Disease Control (CDC) gave a ratio of approximately 1:4, with boys being diagnosed about four times as often as girls.

But are there really four times as many autistic boys and men or just four times as many receiving a diagnosis?

Because of the belief about male-to-female ratios, formal tests for ASD are typically normed on a population that includes more males than females. This means the tests may give more accurate results for boys and men than for girls and women.

Diagnosticians expect that males are far more likely to be autistic than females, so they may look at the same symptoms and attribute them to ASD for males, but not for females.

A study (JAACAP 2017) suggested that the true male-to-female ratio is not as heavily skewed toward males as previously thought and that a diagnostic gender bias appeared to be the cause. The problem this poses is that girls who meet criteria for ASD face a disproportionate risk of not being identified.

Why is it so difficult for autistic girls and women to get a proper diagnosis?

The Mask

For one thing, girls are better able to mask or hide their autistic symptoms than boys are. They watch and imitate other girls so they can figure out what's going on socially. When they're confused or out of their depth, they tend to fade into the background rather than standing out.

When boys fail to figure out social expectations, they often act out in ways that are noticed by parents and teachers. A girl sits quietly watching rather than joining in, and adults assume she is simply shy. It never occurs to them that she is completely baffled by the unwritten social rules of play that all of her peers seem privy to.

When faced with a high-stress, fight-flight-or-freeze situation, such as sensory or social overload, boys usually engage in fight-or-flight, bringing their issues to the attention of parents or teachers. Girls, on the other hand, are more likely to freeze, so no one notices their distress.

Boys flap their hands, and adults wonder if it's a sign of autism. When girls do "jazz hands" or flutter their fingers, people think it's cute.

When they were younger, girls' autistic symptoms went unnoticed, and as they grew older they learned to consciously hide them. Many masked so well that they made it all the way through school and into adulthood without ever being evaluated for ASD. But masking is exhausting. It takes a toll over time, chipping away at self-esteem. They wonder why everyone else seems to float effortlessly through life while they keep running into closed doors. Usually, they are unaware that others don't experience the social and sensory world the way they do. If everyone feels intense pain at certain sounds, and intense anxiety in certain situations, why are all the others able to just keep going as if nothing is wrong? Everyone else must be so strong, and they themselves must be weak. They assume themselves to be flawed, or broken, or defective, rather than understanding that their brains and sensory systems are fundamentally different. They deserve to be identified so that they can better understand themselves.

So, how can we educators and diagnosticians open doors for them when they've been locked out? How can we learn to recognize a condition which has been so well hidden?

The Message

We need to improve our awareness of the different ways autistic girls and women present their symptoms. They really do look different from their male counterparts. The fact that they can mask their symptoms doesn't mean they don't deserve to be properly diagnosed and to receive needed services. It is up to us to look behind the mask and discover the girl who is trying to cover up her autism, or the woman who has successfully hidden her symptoms for decades at the cost of exhaustion, depression, and low self-esteem. They deserve to be seen, recognized, and understood.

In order to get a better understanding of the differences between girls and women who have ASD as compared to those with other, similar conditions, here are seven fictional female figures whose autism was unrecognized until adulthood: shy Cheyenne, Penelope the professor, highly sensitive Akiko, Ruth, who is anxious and depressed, Olivia, who is obsessive and compulsive, Tiffany, an actor on screen and off, and Heidi, who has ADHD. How do each of them meet the criteria for ASD, and how have they flown under the radar to remain undiagnosed for so long? Let's meet them and find out.

 Fictional Female Figures

CHEYENNE

Cheyenne was a bashful baby who did not warm up to new people quickly. She learned to talk a bit early and walked a bit later than many girls her age did, but overall her developmental milestones were met within normal limits. She was always shy, never in the popular clique at school, but she had one best friend. Academics were not a problem, although she never raised her hand in class and remained on the sidelines in group activities. After graduation, although she was nervous about job interviews, she succeeded in finding a job as a library assistant. Cheyenne's husband, her parents, and her one best friend all accept her extreme shyness as part of the sweet person that she is. For most of her life, no one suspected that she was autistic.

PENELOPE

Penelope and Peter were twins, born to their parents later in life. They were welcomed as miracle rainbow babies after many failed attempts to bring a pregnancy to term. Penelope, who rejected the nickname "Penny" as soon as she was able to speak at age eighteen months, was born first. Peter, the younger of the two, was delayed compared to his sister, much more than was to be expected. Before his third birthday, he was diagnosed with autism and began receiving services in the home.

Penelope was in tune with Peter from day one, and she spoke for him when he didn't have the words. She sat in on every therapy session and became a "co-teacher" for her brother. Penelope was the first to notice when he became overly stressed, and she advocated for him with her mother. Eventually they found an in-home teacher who would pay attention to his feelings and let him learn in his own way rather than forcing compliance. Penelope was extremely verbal and precocious, graduating from high school at age 13, earning a BS at 16, an MS at 18, and her first PhD at 23. No one ever suspected that there could be anything wrong with her development or that she, too, might be autistic. Had they looked deeper into her social development rather than focusing on her academic achievement, they would have seen the signs that she kept so well-hidden.

AKIKO

Baby Akiko just couldn't be soothed. She cried often and at length, arching away from her parents as they tried to comfort her. Many things in the environment seemed to set her off, and it took her parents some time to figure out which fabrics, foods, and toys she could tolerate and to control noise levels in the house. In school, she often covered her eyes or her ears and put her head down on her desk. When asked why, she explained that the light hurt her eyes and that the sounds of students working around her hurt her ears. She avoided the other girls and spent her free time reading in the library. Akiko had few friends and remained mostly solitary through high school. The job search was particularly difficult for Akiko, and she felt awkward and like a failure after each interview. She did land several low-level office positions but left each job after a short time. She described the working conditions as intolerable: coworkers eating tuna sandwiches in their cubicles, for example, and the painful sound of the fluorescent lighting overhead and the computer cables in the walls. As an adult, she lives with her parents where she can control her sensory experiences. While everyone who knows her recognizes her extreme sensitivities, no one suspects the more subtle symptoms of ASD which were hidden.

RUTH

Ruth was a quiet, low-key, only child. She rarely smiled or laughed except at certain physical comedy bits or when her dad acted silly in an exaggerated manner. Her facial expression was blank, no matter what she was feeling. Inside, she was afraid of many things and could list each one in order of how terrifying they were: spiders, drowning, heights, dogs, bees, strangers, tsunamis, tapioca pudding, death. She would rather stay home in her room with her familiar toys arranged around her than do anything else. Ruth had an exaggerated fear of typical household sounds. She fell to the ground and curled up in a fetal position each time the doorbell rang, silently waiting for the stranger to go away. If it was a visitor, even a relative or family friend, she ran to her room and stayed there until they left.

Ruth was an expert at worrying. She worried all the time that she would never have a friend, that her parents would die, that she would be alone forever. She used to think that no one at school liked her because she was the only Jewish girl in her class, but then she realized no one liked her in Hebrew School, either. By middle school she had convinced herself that the other girls were stupid and that she did not want friends. By high school her anxiety and depression were finally noticed by a teacher. Although her facial expression never betrayed her inner feelings, she had started cutting herself and was referred to the counselor. She was treated for anxiety and depression, but no one suspected the social confusion and other symptoms of ASD behind the more obvious symptoms of anxiety and depression.

OLIVIA

Olivia was a very fussy baby, and her parents had trouble figuring out why. When she learned to talk, she could tell them what was wrong in her world, and they started to understand some of the things that distressed her. If her sandwich was cut unevenly, if they drove to school by a different route, or if she couldn't get her toy horses to stand in a perfect line without falling down, she would have a meltdown, crying as if her heart was breaking.

In school she annoyingly reminded her teachers if they did anything out of order or in a different way than usual. She pointed out every infraction of every rule, no matter how inconsequential, which made her unpopular with her classmates.

A child psychologist diagnosed her with Obsessive Compulsive Disorder (OCD). He did not go on to ask questions about characteristics of ASD, so Olivia's autism remained undiagnosed for years.

TIFFANY

Tiffany was the best and most beautiful baby in the world, at least according to her parents. Her features were so symmetrical and pleasing that they entered her in "Beautiful Baby" contests whenever an opportunity arose. She caught photographers' eyes and became an infant model for baby food commercials. If she was placed beneath a ceiling fan, she would gaze at it, smiling and cooing, for hours while the photographer worked unnoticed around her. She learned to read at age three and could easily memorize lines and imitate inflections. Tiffany became a child star on television before she was old enough for kindergarten. All she needed was for the director to tell her the line the way it was supposed to be recited, and she could copy the exact vocal inflections perfectly every time, no matter how many takes were needed.

No one noticed that she was unable to make social conversation or use inflections herself. She learned lines and scripts and then used them in her daily life so that she would never have to ad lib. Because she was so compliant and capable, she had a steady career doing small parts and character roles long after her days as a child star were over. Since she never cared about socializing, she was immune to peer pressure. Her parents were very protective of her and never let her take a meeting alone or go out unsupervised. This suited Tiffany to a T. Eventually, though, she wondered why she always felt like a guest star in her own life, unable to function without a script.

HEIDI

Heidi was active since before birth, keeping her mother awake prenatally with near-constant kicking and turning. She was a loud and active baby with no fear of climbing, new people, new foods, or risky activities. In school, it was difficult for her to focus on the teacher because of her strong interest in the world around her. She was diagnosed with ADHD, and her teachers realized that she learned best if she could be in motion while learning, bouncing, jiggling, fiddling, and rocking. She was athletic and excelled in individual rather than team sports, as she often failed to pay attention to the group plan and impulsively went her own way. Friendship was challenging for her, as she often came on too strong and put people off. She sometimes stared closely at people's eyeballs, and she sometimes asked a new person long lists of personal questions, one after the other, rarely pausing to hear the answers. The other girls thought she was "weird" and avoided her.

Heidi struggled with time management in college, but with support from her parents she eventually finished an AA in five years. She found a job as a mail carrier, a career that suited her need to be on the go and work outdoors. She loved meeting the people and pets on her route. Customers who were not put off by her exuberance appreciated her spontaneous, positive energy. She was often reprimanded by her superiors, though, for complaints from customers and coworkers who felt that her straightforward, to-the-point communication was harsh and disrespectful. She herself was clueless about these incidents and worried that she would be fired and never understand why. Heidi's symptoms of ADHD were so strong and visible, everyone assumed that her social awkwardness, communication mishaps, and executive function struggles were due entirely to her ADHD. In fact, that was the tip of the iceberg, and her many symptoms of ASD were overlooked.

Real-life counterparts of these fictional female figures can be found in schools and communities everywhere. Their parents, their teachers, and the professionals they turn to for help often do not see the hidden signs of autism, and so they go unrecognized. In addition to cisgender women, there are many transgender women and nonbinary folk, and even men, who have learned to successfully mask their characteristics of autism as a survival strategy. They all deserve to be seen and recognized.

In the chapters that follow, we'll see how each of these girls meets the DSM-5 diagnostic criteria for ASD and how they have managed to avoid being recognized. The *Behind the Mask* sections offer specific questions diagnosticians may ask to bring to light the subtle symptoms of autism that women have hidden so successfully and for so long. *In Her Own Words* gives voice to actually autistic people who are willing to share their stories so that others may learn.

In Her Own Words

"I have spent 51 years leading a double life, and it has come at a great cost to me both physically and emotionally. Most people wake in the morning, brush their teeth, eat breakfast, and go into the world as themselves. I, on the other hand, must get into character, fight off the daily nausea that comes with overwhelming anxiety, and steel myself for another day. Eight-plus hours on the stage that most people call daily life. If I were to look at it from an optimistic point of view, I would say I'm very lucky to be so successful at passing for what people consider 'normal.' The problem with playing a character really well is that it is emotionally and physically exhausting, and it's not sustainable. A person might possibly keep such a secret hidden if they lived alone, but keeping up their character in public AND at home is an impossibility!"

— *Shanda K, age 51*

PART I
SOCIAL COMMUNICATION AND INTERACTION

"Persistent deficits in social communication and social interaction . . ."

> — *Diagnostic and Statistical Manual for Mental Disorders, Fifth Edition (DSM-5)*

"Social thinking skills must be directly taught to children and adults with ASD. Doing so opens doors of social understandings in all areas of life."

> — *Dr. Temple Grandin, autistic author, speaker, professor*

Chapter One

RECIPROCITY
A Two-Way Street

"Deficits in social-emotional reciprocity...from abnormal social approach and failure of normal back-and-forth conversation; to reduced sharing of interests, emotions, or affect; to failure to initiate or respond to social interactions."

— *Diagnostic and Statistical Manual for Mental Disorders, Fifth Edition (DSM 5)*

"There is more to autism than the narrow representations we are often shown."

— *Kay Kerr, autistic author*

Reciprocity is defined as a state of mutual dependence, the act of exchanging things with others for the benefit of both parties. It may be a social practice of responding to an act of kindness by a return of kindness. In conversation, we reciprocate by asking and answering questions, commenting on statements, and letting our conversational partner know we are with them by nodding or vocalizing such as "Mm hm," or "Uh huh."

Social reciprocity refers to the back-and-forth flow of social interaction, whether verbal or nonverbal. The behavior of one person influences another, who is influenced in turn. It may include colleagues working together on a task or children playing the same game together, each one understanding what roles each of them plays. When a baby claps their hands after seeing someone smile and clap for them, when a toddler waves back in response to a wave, when two preschoolers play house, they are engaging in social reciprocity.

Social reciprocity also includes sharing smiles, offering comfort, asking for help, playing or working cooperatively in groups, and both initiating and responding to social overtures. The manner in which girls and women with ASD engage in these activities of social reciprocity is different from that of their typical peers in ways that can be difficult to recognize. Read about our fictional female figures to understand social reciprocity from their perspective.

Fictional Female Figures

CHEYENNE

Cheyenne is never the first to reach out to new people. Even her grandparents must wait patiently each time they visit until she feels comfortable enough to approach them. As a baby in the shopping cart, if a person behind them in line made eye contact with her, she turned her face toward her mother and hid her eyes. Most shy children might hesitantly peek out to make brief eye contact with the other person and then quickly duck back, hiding a shy smile, but Cheyenne never looked back. As a toddler and preschooler, when there was another child her age at a park, her mother would point them out and ask Cheyenne if she might like to play with them. Cheyenne only hid behind her mother or put her hands over her face. She never peeked out at them from behind her mother or showed any curiosity or interest, as a typical shy child might. In school, she did not approach others to join in their play, and she ran away if others invited her to play with them. Because everyone knew she was shy, no one suspected that her lack of reciprocity was a characteristic of autism rooted in confusion about social interactions and expectations. They thought she was just shy Cheyenne, keeping to herself.

PENELOPE

Penelope didn't chat, she lectured.

In preschool she explained to her teachers that insects and bugs were not synonymous, and while all bugs are insects, all insects are not bugs. They assumed she was babbling nonsense.

In kindergarten she corrected her teacher who called a dimetrodon a dinosaur, pointing out that dimetrodons shared more characteristics with mammals than with dinosaurs, and she was scolded for talking back and making things up.

At no point did she try to engage in reciprocal back-and-forth social conversation with others. People were clearly so ill-informed about even the most basic scientific facts that it was hopeless to even try to educate them. She focused instead on getting through the school system as fast as humanly possible.

The only time Penelope engaged in any kind of reciprocity was with her brother. The two of them enjoyed lots of social play together, such as holding hands and leaning back and forth while singing, "Row, row, row your boat," for hours on end. It didn't look like the kind of typical play of most siblings, but it was clear that the twins loved each other. They had a secret, nonverbal language for the two of them alone, and no one else was permitted into their club.

AKIKO

Akiko never knew the right thing to say; the logical thing seemed to be to say nothing unless asked a specific question. As a toddler, she didn't speak at all until she was three, and then she suddenly began speaking in complete sentences. As a child, if another girl told her she had a pretty dress or that they liked her doll, she said nothing. They hadn't asked her a question, so what was there to say? The other girls soon decided she was stuck up. They never invited her to birthday parties, but she didn't realize she was being excluded. In high school she figured out that people expect you to say something when they talk to you, even if there is no direct question to answer. When a boy paid her a compliment, she said, "I know," and was called conceited. When a girl in her gym class twisted her ankle and fell while running

6

laps, Akiko happened to be the closest one to her. As the girl cried in pain, Akiko was filled with intense pain herself. Her own ankle ached in response to being so close to her classmate's pain. Her heart went out to this girl on the ground, but she had no way to show her feelings. She longed to be helpful in some way. What should she do? What would she want if she were the one with the twisted ankle? Akiko knew she preferred to be alone when injured, to wait for the pain to subside in privacy. She stood and looked at the crying girl from about six feet away, with no facial expression, and then she did the most compassionate thing she could think of: she walked away, her heart aching with pity and shared pain. Her reputation as a stuck-up, conceited, cold-hearted robot was now carved in stone.

RUTH

Social conversation never made sense to Ruth; it seemed to her that everyone else got a script, but she was ad-libbing. Once, when the other girls were talking about their favorite cartoon, she was reminded of her favorite scene from a Marx Brothers movie. She could clearly see it in her mind, and she suddenly shouted, "It wasn't a mirror! It was Harpo!" and started laughing loudly. The girls told her she was crazy, and her laughter dissolved into tears. In high school, she tried to observe and imitate other girls in conversation so that she could fit in. At the beginning of one conversation, she thought of something to add that was relevant to the discussion, and she planned how to say it so they wouldn't think she was stupid. After carefully crafting her sentence in her head, she looked for an opening to get her words in, but the conversation was bouncing back and forth faster than she could keep up. It reminded her of trying to run into Double Dutch jump ropes: the ropes kept turning, and if you didn't time it right, they would hit you. Finally, the girls were laughing about something, so there was a gap in the conversation. Quickly before she missed her opportunity, Ruth blurted out her scripted sentence as fast as she could, words running together. She was met with silence and blank stares. Apparently, the conversation topic had changed several times since she had planned her appropriate comment. Now her greatest fear was realized: she looked like an idiot. She was an idiot. She replayed her humiliation in her mind again and again but could see no way to fix it. She was just broken.

OLIVIA

As a toddler, Olivia did not show much interest in other babies and seemed to find them distasteful. She avoided the other preschoolers the way she avoided finger painting: completely and without exception. Olivia rarely reached out to other children to play and usually walked around the perimeter of the playground throughout recess. On the rare occasions that others asked her to play, she appeared oblivious to their social overtures, so they soon gave up. She attended college online and found that she learned much better in the absence of other students. Living alone and working from home gave her freedom from the obligatory back-and-forth social nonsense that the rest of the world seemed to expect. She was happiest when she could control all of the variables in her world, so the idea of social reciprocity was not important to her.

TIFFANY

Tiffany learned early on that if she smiled and looked down demurely, occasionally glancing back up so that her thick eyelashes fluttered above her blue eyes, people would not have many other expectations. If she didn't start a conversation, others were happy to talk to her and always told her what a wonderful listener she was. If she was asked a question that she did not have a scripted answer for, she found that a slight giggle and the tiniest of shrugs, accompanied by a small smile and raised eyebrows, were sufficient. She was so lovely to look at that no one cared if she didn't talk much, and she considered this a saving grace, since she never knew what to say.

HEIDI

Heidi was always on the go and interested in everything. As a baby, while her mother waited in line at the grocery store, she was intent on climbing out of her cart to reach out to the other people in the store. She stared at them, squealing in delight as if they were the most fascinating things she had ever seen. Often it was their glasses or cap or earrings that caught her attention rather than the person wearing them. As a toddler and preschooler, when the family went to the park, she strained to get out of her car seat so she could run to where the other kids were playing. Her parents thought she was interested in the other children, but in fact she was more interested in climbing on the playground equipment than she was in playing with the other kids. At times she even stepped on them as she climbed to the top, seemingly oblivious that it was a child she was stepping on rather than just another rung on the ladder. Sometimes she rushed straight to another child she saw, but once she got there, it was the toy the child held that was the most interesting. In high school, she wanted to be friends with everyone and didn't realize that there was a social pecking order. She eventually got tired of approaching popular groups and being brushed off, insulted, or ignored. She joined the track team and spent her breaks running laps to avoid the confusing social maze that she could never seem to get through. Later, in her job as a mail carrier, she often used inappropriate social approaches, such as asking what was inside the unmarked brown boxes she delivered. She eventually learned that it is okay to ask the ages of children and dogs, but not adults. Unfortunately, each time she learned a new rule for what is or is not socially appropriate when approaching others, she used it only in that specific situation and did not generalize to a broader awareness of the give and take of social reciprocity.

Behind the Mask

Each of these seven girls struggled with social reciprocity in their own way. For each, the struggle began in early childhood and continued to adulthood. In every case, their deficits were misunderstood and their autism was not recognized.

The obvious first step in determining if a girl or woman meets the criteria for reciprocity is to observe and learn about her social approaches, conversations, and interactions. But will this give you a full picture of the girl or woman you're assessing? Not necessarily. Often, when girls fail to approach others socially, they are seen as shy rather than autistic. Here are some important questions to consider:

> ➢ Rather than approaching someone else, does she usually wait for the other person to talk to her first, or to ask her out, or to take the first step in starting up a friendship?

> ➢ Does she try to initiate conversations or friendships only to realize that she comes on too strong and puts people off, or that her intentions are misunderstood?

> ➢ Is she quiet in groups because she doesn't understand or easily follow the social conversation?

> ➢ Does she require a longer pause before she feels she can say something, but there never seems to be a pause large enough for her to be certain it's her turn to talk?

➢ Does she raise her hand to speak in informal conversations, even though others find it quirky or odd?

➢ In school, was there another girl who took her under her wing to help her navigate social situations? (Or did she wish someone had, because she needed it?)

➢ Does she imitate others, smiling or laughing when they smile or laugh, all the while hoping no one realizes she doesn't really know what's going on socially?

➢ Does she tend to keep her feelings or interests to herself because she has learned that trying to share personal things usually goes wrong for her?

➢ If she tends to play alone at recess or to avoid social invitations after work, why is this? Are social situations stressful or too uncertain and unpredictable?

➢ Does she seem not to notice if someone says hello to her, as if she is in a daze and doesn't hear them?

Any of these characteristics may be true for girls or women who are not on the spectrum, but when there are a significant number of symptoms of autism hiding behind their mask, it's time to take a closer look.

In Her Own Words

"I do want to talk and interact, but I struggle with the basic necessities of social interaction that come naturally to other people (eye contact, laughing at an appropriate time, body language, etc.) I often find myself completely at a loss as to how to carry on a conversation, especially with new people. I will try to keep them talking about themselves, as this seems to make most people comfortable, and it takes the pressure off of me to reciprocate. There is a constant dialogue going on in my mind as I talk myself through every social interaction: What do I ask next? What is a socially acceptable response to that question? Am I oversharing, or not sharing enough? Do I come off as too friendly, or uptight? I suspect this is a significant factor to the exhaustion I feel in social situations. It's not that I would rather be alone than accept an invitation; it's a matter of energy allowance. Will I have enough time to recover and rest afterwards? Using mental energy to work through each step of a social engagement quickly uses up this limited resource, and then functioning becomes difficult and rest is necessary. I try to carefully plan out social events with the support of my spouse and family so that I can enjoy the experience as much as possible and be present in the way they need me to be. Autism demands balance and careful consideration, but it doesn't mean that I have to miss out on life's experiences with my loved ones."

— *Jessica Dawn, diagnosed at age 33*

Chapter Two

NONVERBAL COMMUNICATION

You Don't Say

"Deficits in nonverbal communicative behaviors used for social interaction, ranging, for example, from poorly integrated verbal and nonverbal communication; to abnormalities in eye contact and body language or deficits in understanding and use of gestures; to a total lack of facial expression and nonverbal communication."

> — *Diagnostic and Statistical Manual for Mental Disorders, Fifth Edition (DSM-5)*

"If I look away from you while you are speaking to me, it means I am listening intently."

> — *Michelle Dorothy Riksman, autistic author, artist, and photographer*

N onverbal communication is a huge part of human interactions. It's much more than the obvious: smiling, nodding and shaking the head, pointing, shrugging, and giving looks of obvious surprise (mouth open, eyebrows raised) or anger (mouth tight and turned down, eyebrows lowered significantly.) It's also the many small and subtle micro-expressions that indicate not only happiness, sadness, fear, and anger, but also emotions that are more difficult to read, such as disgust, contempt, and confusion. When boys have an extremely flat affect, showing no emotion, it may raise a red flag noticed by parents and teachers. Most of the boys at play show a wide range of expressions, so the autistic boy stands out. Girls, on the other hand, are expected to be less outward in their expressions, and extreme subtlety may be seen as being subdued, mature, and ladylike, but not autistic.

Eye contact is an obvious indicator, and many assessors heavily weight the presence or absence of eye contact when making diagnostic decisions. According to the DSM-5, as long as the proper number of items meets criteria, there is no one behavior that would automatically rule out or rule in autism. Many girls and women do make eye contact or fake it well, and sometimes it is indistinguishable at face value from the eye contact made by their neurotypical peers. But there's often more to the story. Instead of simply noting whether eye contact was observed, ask how eye contact feels to them. Uncomfortable? Exhausting? Invasive? Painful? Ask about their early experiences with people saying, "Look at me!" Did they teach themselves to make or fake eye contact at some point in an effort to blend in because they realized it was expected? Do they focus on the speaker's mouth, or forehead, or the bridge of their nose, to try to simulate eye contact without actually looking at the eyes? Perhaps they have a special routine for eye contact, such as looking at the eyes for five seconds, looking away for three seconds, and then making five more seconds of eye contact. They may be constantly counting the seconds in their head, looking away, looking back, all the while trying to simultaneously carry on a conversation. It sounds exhausting, doesn't it?

For many, trying to integrate verbal and nonverbal communication is difficult. If you ask them to both show (with gestures or pantomime) and tell you how to do something, they may prefer to do one at a time. Perhaps they can integrate the two, but it takes some much longer, with many hesitations as they try to plan how to talk and move their hands at the same time.

Difficulty integrating verbal and nonverbal is often especially true with eye contact. Many people cannot look at a person while talking or listening to them. Some students have told teachers, "I can either look at you or I can listen to you, but not both. Which do you want from me?"

When boys don't understand the nonverbal component of a communication, they are often open about their confusion. You can tell by their reaction that they didn't get it. Girls, on the other hand, are much better at masking, mirroring others, and pretending they understand when they really don't.

Each of our fictional female figures struggled with nonverbal communication in one way or another, but their struggles were never recognized as symptomatic of autism.

Fictional Female Figures

CHEYENNE

When Cheyenne looked down and avoided eye contact, everyone chalked it up to her extreme shyness. It seemed to fit with her personality that she rarely gestured when she spoke, but rather kept her hands clasped tightly together in front of her. If she forgot a word, she froze up, gestured silently and ineffectively for a moment, and then quickly gave up and shook her head. Putting together words and gestures did not come naturally to her, but no one in her life suspected that this could be due to autism.

PENELOPE

Linguistics was so valued by Penelope that the concept of trying to communicate nonverbally was anathema to her, outside of the bond she shared with her brother. Staring at another human's eyeballs or moving one's hands while speaking was an activity she considered nonsensical and therefore not something she engaged in. She could be recognized from across campus by her unique walk, head down, arms motionless, leaning slightly forward while taking great strides to get to her next class with no time wasted. When meeting with groups of students or teaching assistants, she had learned to loudly bark the last name of the person she was addressing before beginning the stream of information she had to impart to them. She developed this practice after a colleague told her that when she kept her head down all the time, no one knew who she was talking to, and most were afraid to ask.

AKIKO

Because she wore dark glasses most of the time, no one realized the extent to which Akiko avoided eye contact. People in her life understood her extreme sensitivity to light, among other sensitivities, and they didn't even think about whether or not she was making eye contact behind her shades. On the rare occasions when she spoke, she moved her hands gracefully through the air, like butterflies. Everyone found this charming and never noticed that her gestures were lovely, but not at all communicative.

RUTH

Early on, Ruth figured out that people expect you to look at their eyes, and if you don't, they have negative thoughts about you. She found it quite disturbing to actually look right at an eyeball, wet and quivery, moving slightly all the time. It made her queasy, but she forced herself to do it when she had to. Teachers assumed you couldn't hear them if you weren't looking at their eyeballs, which was patently ridiculous. We hear with our ears, not our eyes. Looking at the teacher made her head hurt and her ears buzz, and she couldn't understand what they were saying. If she looked down or closed her eyes, she could understand the words, but as soon as the teacher said, "Ruth, look at me!" she knew the rest of the lecture would be a complete loss.

OLIVIA

Olivia never really understood what people meant by their gestures and the ways they held their bodies. Oh, she knew that a head nodding up and down meant yes, and a head shaking from side to side meant no, but there were a lot of other things she wasn't sure about, so she researched gestures online. She learned that when someone shrugs their shoulders, raising them up toward their ears, it was supposed to mean that they didn't understand something. Shrugging means "I don't know." It seemed simple and straightforward, but like so many things she thought she understood, it wasn't. Once in middle school she was waiting with other students to go into English, and one girl said to another, "You didn't even read the book? Oooh, you're in for it now!" The girl she was talking to sighed, brushed her hair out of her eyes, and shrugged a shoulder. The shrug should have meant that she didn't understand the saying, so Olivia explained for her. "When she said, 'You're in for it now,' she meant that you're in for a failing grade. You should have read the book because the test is today. That's what she meant." The other girls looked at her like she was an alien and said some very rude words to her before turning their backs to her. Was she an alien? Sometimes she wondered. And other times she was sure that she was.

TIFFANY

Whenever someone looked into her eyes, Tiffany felt immediately vulnerable and frightened. As she grew up and moved from her early career as a child actor on a popular television series to being offered more adult roles such as romantic leads, she withdrew. Her parents understood her hesitance and told her agent that she would only consider supporting roles, such as the best friend of the leading lady. Being directed to gaze longingly into an actor's eyes was something she could not even think about. It was easy to look at a camera and to look past the other actors in a group scene, but close-up two-shots were intolerable for her. Although her agent didn't understand and thought she was making a mistake, Tiffany was much more content to have a modest but steady career playing small roles if it meant she could avoid making eye contact with a leading man.

HEIDI

A lot of people talk with their hands, but Heidi was unique. When she talked, her hands waved and gesticulated wildly, but not necessarily in a communicative manner. A constant grin was her default setting, and she had very few other facial expressions. When under stress, her smile just got bigger and more fixed. She often looked deeply into someone's eyes, holding the stare for too long without realizing the other person was uncomfortable. For Heidi, being able to see herself in the reflective mirror of a person's eyes was endlessly fascinating. While staring at eyes, the world around her seemed to fade, and she never quite heard what the person was saying to her. At the end, when her parent or teacher said, "Do you understand?" she would echo, "Understand." Then the adult would say, "Good," and leave her alone. Heidi was never sure why she later got in trouble for doing something that they said they had just talked to her about. Punishments seemed arbitrary.

Behind the Mask

Our fictional female figures each had difficulty with nonverbal communication, whether expressing it, understanding it receptively, or integrating it with their verbal communication.

When looking at the DSM-5 criterion regarding nonverbal communication, here are several questions to consider.

➢ Is she able to gesture and talk at the same time? Ask her to act out some simple, everyday task and describe what she's doing simultaneously. Can she show and tell you what she is doing at the same time? Is there a long pause while she thinks about it? Does she first mime the action without talking, and then tell what the action was without gesturing, rather than integrating them?

➢ Can she integrate eye contact with talking or listening, or must she look away or close her eyes if she wants to really hear and understand verbal information? In class, did she find that every time the teacher said, "Look at me," she then could not comprehend or remember what they said to her?

➤ Perhaps you observe that she makes eye contact with you. Don't assume that this is easy or natural for her, but probe further:

➤ What does eye contact feel like to her? Invasive, uncomfortable, stressful, painful, unnecessarily distracting, or just plain weird?

➤ Does she recall teaching herself to make eye contact when she realized that people expect it?

➤ Does she understand what people mean by their gestures, facial expressions, or body language? Does she tend to negatively misinterpret others' nonverbal expressions, assuming someone is mad at them when maybe they're simply tired?

➤ Does she tend to have a bland, neutral expression most of the time? Have people often told her to cheer up when she was perfectly content, or asked her to smile when she thought she was already smiling? Have people asked her why she was upset when she wasn't upset at all?

Questions such as these can help the assessor look behind the mask to recognize the hidden autistic-like behaviors and characteristics that may be easily missed by most.

"Facial expressions are hard for me. I am not good at reading people's expressions, because sometimes if someone is tired then they might have an angry face, but that doesn't mean they're really angry. I have to ask what people are expressing because otherwise I just assume I did something wrong. I also have trouble making eye contact with people I do not know. I am better at normal conversation when I am talking to people I know, but if it is a serious conversation that requires a lot of intonations and emotional expressions and other complex dynamics, then I will struggle to speak and make eye contact. I always try to time how long I stare into people's eyes before I look away. It doesn't always work so well. I am still figuring it out."

— *Nakeba Todd*

Chapter Three

RELATIONSHIPS
It's Peopley Out There

"Deficits in developing, maintaining, and understanding relationships, ranging, for example, from difficulty adjusting behavior to suit various social contexts; to difficulties in sharing imaginative play or in making friends; to absence of interest in peers."

— *Diagnostic and Statistical Manual for Mental Disorders, Fifth Edition (DSM-5)*

"A formal diagnosis has undoubtedly changed my life. I now understand why I found it so hard to make friends as a young person, and why I often chose solitude. I always assumed it was just because I was shy."

— *Madge Woollard, autistic pianist*

The *Oxford Learner's Dictionary* defines *relationship* as "the way in which two people, groups or countries behave towards each other or deal with each other." Relationships of all kinds have been challenging for autistic people. This can range from a lack of interest in relationships entirely to an intense desire for relationship which may not be realized. Attempts to reach out and connect socially are often thwarted by a basic misunderstanding of the social nuances required. It's often neither easy nor natural for neurodivergent people to successfully navigate the murky waters of acquaintances, work colleagues, friendship, and more intimate relationships.

Many people with autism generalize their behaviors across settings in ways that are not always seen as appropriate by their neurotypical peers. They may act the same whether they are in a theater, in a bar, in a place of worship, or at a baby shower. They may talk to people with the same tone or attitude, whether they are talking to a pal or a professor, their buddy or their boss. There is no handbook that describes how or why people show different affect and actions in different social situations. Most people intuitively know, but not autists. It can be worse for women and girls on the spectrum, because society expects them to be more socially savant than the guys are and judges them more harshly when they fall short of expectations. They are often treated as if their awkwardness were purposeful rudeness and are shunned rather than shown a different way to behave.

Making friends is difficult, and when there is a friendship, it can be fragile. Our girls on the spectrum usually don't know how to start up, maintain, or keep a friendship, and many friendships are short-lived. There can be misunderstandings and breakups. Many autistic women negatively misinterpret subtle or nonverbal communications and assume their friend or date must be mad at them when they were only tired or distracted. Once something goes wrong and there is an argument or hurt feelings, that often means the end forever, as our girls on the spectrum frequently lack the skills necessary to repair a broken friendship.

Struggles with relationships usually start early in school days and continue through to adulthood. When the other girls are playing house or pretending to be teachers or fashion designers, our girls on the spectrum may have little interest or ability to make believe in the same way. They often prefer arranging their fashion dolls' outfits and accessories and organizing them by color and have no interest in pretending their doll is getting ready to go on a date. They miss opportunities for social practice that the other girls acquire through play.

Many autistic girls find that other girls their age are not particularly interesting, and they can't relate to them. Some view other children as fascinating but foreign subjects that they want to study. Some completely ignore other children as irrelevant or not very relatable. Many prefer the company of teachers, librarians, and other adults over that of their peers. Others will happily play with much younger children or hang out with the boys rather than the girls.

Any one of these relationship challenges may not be diagnostic in and of itself but may be part of a bigger pattern of autistic behaviors that can go unnoticed. Let's see how each of our fictional female figures coped with relationships.

Fictional Female Figures

CHEYENNE

"BFF" is how Cheyenne would describe Bethany, the daughter of her parents' best friends. The two families had been close since before the girls were born, and they were more like cousins than friends. Bethany was naturally quiet and slightly shy herself and often acted as a "little mother hen" for Cheyenne in social situations. If only they had attended the same elementary school, those years would have been easier for Cheyenne. Her reticence to initiate or respond to social overtures continued throughout her school years, college, and the workplace, so she was usually alone. When Bethany fell in love, she introduced Cheyenne to her fiancé's brother. Gabe was painfully shy, a self-described computer geek. The four of them often spent time hanging out together. Eventually Cheyenne and Gabe grew to feel comfortable in one another's company, and friendship blossomed into love. Not long after Bethany's big church wedding, Cheyenne and Gabe married quietly in the courthouse. Gabe understood, appreciated, and loved her exactly the way she was, and she had grown to love and trust him, too. Fate (and Bethany) had brought love to Cheyenne, despite her extreme reticence and discomfort with most social relationships.

PENELOPE

Penelope did not suffer fools gladly, and compared to her, everyone else was a fool. She did not seek friendship, only scholarship. Her colleagues considered her an "odd duck," her students made fun of her privately, and her assistants were terrified of her. The only relationship that meant anything to her was her brother, Peter. From infancy, during childhood, and throughout their entire lives, the twins were each other's worlds. For Penelope, the only logical reasons for doing anything were pursuing knowledge and making Peter's life easier and happier. She pursued career advancement because the raise in pay allowed her to provide the things that he needed and enjoyed. It was enough.

AKIKO

Solitude suited Akiko, who had few friends from elementary through high school. Everyone else seemed to understand hidden social rules, while she remained clueless. She had a friend in second grade for a while, but it didn't last long. One day the other girl got mad, and Akiko had no idea why. The friendship ended like a door slamming shut, and Akiko never even tried to open it to find out what went wrong. When she was a teenager, her parents and aunts tried to set her up by having parties with their friends' children her age, hoping she would find a friend. Instead, she usually retreated to her room. The boys smelled of sweat and the girls smelled of perfume, and their chattering, with multiple conversations against a backdrop of music, clinking ice in glasses, and people chewing, was impossible to handle. If putting up with that nightmare was the price of relationships, then Akiko wanted nothing to do with it.

RUTH

Saturday morning cartoons made friendship look easy, and Ruth yearned for a friend of her own. When she started school, she believed that she would finally have a friend, like the magical ponies she loved on TV. Starting on the first day of school, she waited patiently for someone to come up to her and say, "Will you be my friend?" All morning she imagined which little girl might be her first friend. At recess she stood at the edge of the play yard waiting for that girl to ask her to play, but it never happened. She grew more and more sad and listless, waiting and waiting for the magic of friendship. Finally, she decided that it was up to her to make it happen. Each morning, she decided which girl would be her friend and what they would play together. Today, it would be Maria on the swings. She bravely approached Maria and asked if she wanted to swing, but Maria was jumping rope and said no. All recess she waited for Maria to go to the swings so she could join her there, but it didn't happen. Day after day, Ruth made a friendship plan in her head, and day after day she stood alone at the edge of the playground, watching the other friends playing, waiting for the perfect friendship moment. Eventually she gave up and found solitary things to do during recess.

As an adult, Ruth met a woman who shared many of her interests, and it seemed that they would be great friends. They texted every few days and got together for coffee about once a month. Then one day, she realized they hadn't spoken or texted in over six months. Had it been her turn to initiate contact? Was her friend mad at her? After such a long time, Ruth had no idea what to do or say, so she let the friendship slip away without ever knowing why.

OLIVIA

Olivia did not have friends in school. When asked who her best friends were, she listed the librarian, the school secretary, her teacher, and the cafeteria lady by name, but no one her own age. When pressed to name more, she listed every child in her classroom in alphabetical order, with no apparent understanding of the difference between a classmate and a friend. Her classmates as a group all seemed to dislike her. They called her "Teacher's Pest" and booed whenever she pointed out another rule infraction or reminded the teacher to give them homework. Olivia asked her mother what "Teacher's Pest" meant, and her mother said it was probably word play for "Teacher's Pet." Olivia knew she was not a pet, she was a human, so her mother explained that a teacher's pet is the teacher's favorite. This sounded like a compliment to Olivia. So why the mismatch between her classmates' kind words and their angry tone of voice and mean facial expressions? She ultimately decided it was one more reason to avoid other children, who were clearly mentally challenged and beneath her interest.

After high school, Olivia spent one night in the dorm with a roommate, and then moved back home to her own room and continued her education online. Dating was never of interest to her, and the idea of being intimate with a man seemed gross and disturbing. She was much happier in her own space, where no one else could rearrange her things or impose their expectations on her.

TIFFANY

An on-set classroom with the actors playing her siblings was Tiffany's only school experience. They all did their daily lessons with tutors and parents close at hand, and then they were back on the set as soon as child labor laws allowed. Tiffany enjoyed pretending to have friends and brothers and sisters as long as they had scripts to follow. There was little time to socialize, and her parents did not encourage her to go out with her costars as a naive teenager, so her experience of being and having a friend was entirely make-believe.

Much later, as an adult, she began reaching out to other actors she'd worked with that she felt a kinship with, those who were quirky, or quiet, or shy when they weren't acting. The ones she felt closest to, with whom she found understanding and friendship, were often neurodivergent. These were successful people in the arts, and their fans probably had no idea they had different brains because they played their roles so well. Tiffany didn't realize that her natural affinity for them was because she, herself, was on the autism spectrum.

There were five who became particularly close friends. They called themselves the Vladimir Hinks Society of Good Quirks and always met secretly and in disguise, far from paparazzi and fans. It was such a blessed relief for them to just be themselves in one another's company that they met four times a year, choosing their locations in the off seasons to avoid crowds. Each winter they exchanged holiday gifts which must cost no more than one dollar. The year that Tiffany gave everyone small strings of twinkling fairy lights from a one-dollar store, her gift was a huge hit.

One of Tiffany's favorite memories of her group of odd friends was the time that their senior (and most famous) friend left their booth in a little diner and wandered into the kitchen. When he returned and they asked what he'd been up to, he said that they seemed short-handed, so he'd pitched in to wash the dishes. The idea that a world-famous, award-winning actor would just pop into the kitchen and start washing dishes tickled Tiffany, and she laughed again every time she remembered it.

Tiffany's parents had driven her to auditions and to the set for work her entire life. The idea of learning to drive herself made her extremely anxious, and each time they brought it up, she hyperventilated. They stopped pushing her to get her license, but they also knew that they wouldn't live forever, so eventually they hired a driver for her. Tiffany sat silently through each interview, and after the applicants left, she usually shook her head slightly and looked down. The idea of being in a car with someone she didn't know was scary.

Finally her parents chose Danny, the son of one of their friends. Danny was putting himself through college, so a job where he could do homework while waiting for Tiffany was perfect. All he needed to do was drive Tiffany to and from the studio and any other appointments she had, and be available to run errands as needed. At first her mother rode with her in the backseat until Tiffany became accustomed to seeing the back of Danny's head while he drove. He finished his BA majoring in business and minoring in psychology, then his MBA, all while waiting for Tiffany. Her parents kept raising his pay so that he wouldn't leave her, and he was happy to stay.

Over the years Tiffany became more and more comfortable with Danny. She enjoyed hearing about his studies, and he loved to hear her talk about the things that interested her. She was the kindest and most purely good human he had ever met, and he felt privileged to help make her life easier.

One day her phone rang, and she stared at it in abject horror. Danny glanced over and saw that the call was from a major talk show host.

"Are you going to answer that?" he asked. She shook her head in silent horror. "Are you sure?" Tiffany mutely handed the phone to him as if it were a sleeping tarantula. Danny answered, "Good morning, this is Tiffany Grant's personal assistant, how may I help you? ...You want Miss Grant to do an interview on your show? Let me check." He raised his eyebrows at her and she covered her mouth with both hands and stared wide-eyed back at him. "Do you want to do it?" he whispered.

She lowered her hands to whisper back, "Which character do they want me to be?" Danny relayed the information, and the word came back that they wanted the actor, Tiffany Grant, being herself, not acting as one of her characters. She shook her head violently. "I don't know how to do that! I don't know who that is!"

Danny said he would have to get back to them later, and he talked her through her concerns. She adored watching this talk show host on TV and would love to meet him, but she was petrified of being asked questions she didn't have a script for.

After some negotiation, Danny sent the talk show a list of questions Tiffany would be happy to be asked. They sent more that they wanted to ask her, and an agreement was made. Danny helped her write scripts for each question, and she practiced her answers. When the time came, she was poised and appeared relaxed, and the host was thoroughly charmed by her. Pretending to be an actor on a talk show and delivering pre-planned lines worked for her.

Fifteen years of driving Tiffany and being her right-hand man, protecting her from the parts of the world that were difficult for her, had been an honor and a privilege for Danny. Eventually, though, he realized that he had fallen in love with her. He finally decided to tell her how he felt, but not as an employee.

"Tiffany, I want you to fire me."

"No, I don't want to! Why would I?"

"Because I need to speak to you, not to my boss. Just to you."

"Are you quitting? Aren't you happy?"

"Just fire me temporarily, and then after I say my piece, you can hire me back again, and I'll say yes." After she agreed, he told her about his feelings for her, that he was in love with her and it wouldn't be right to feel that way and keep it a secret.

As it turned out, Tiffany had similar feelings that she didn't know how to express. She hadn't imagined that he would feel the same, so her feelings had remained hidden.

After talking with her parents, since she had never made a major decision without asking their counsel, the two were married quietly and secretly in a courthouse, with only her parents as their witnesses. He didn't know much about autism other than what he'd learned in his psych courses, and as yet no one realized that Tiffany was autistic, but Danny knew her. He had spent over 15 years watching her, learning what kinds of things would cause her stress or bring her joy. She had needed time to process her feelings for him, but now she knew that what she felt was love and trust. She felt safe being herself with Danny, as she did with the Vladimir Hinks Society of Good Quirks. It was lovely to find her people, and she cherished them.

HEIDI

Friendship was challenging for Heidi, as she often came on too strong, putting people off. She sometimes stared at people's eyeballs and often asked intrusive questions. The other girls at school thought she was weird and avoided her. On the playground, she often ran to join a group of kids playing ball, but then grabbed the ball and ran off to play with it alone, not realizing the chaos she left behind her until the yard duty supervisor caught up with her and made her sit on the bench. Heidi spent a lot of recesses on the bench until her teacher realized how disruptive she was in the afternoons when she wasn't allowed to run and play. Eventually they let her bring her own ball from home so that she wouldn't disrupt the others' games. In high school she often approached groups and asked pointed, awkward questions until she was shunned. She was just trying to get to know people, but she was doing it wrong. Heidi figured out that the social hierarchy was everybody else at the top, while she was at the bottom. Later, in her job as a mail carrier, she tried making friends, but it never worked out. If someone on her route was friendly, smiled and said hello, she interpreted this as the first stage of developing a friendship. She never quite understood why she was always rejected when she followed up the friendly greeting with a suggestion that they get together for a beer later. Her limited understanding of social relationships got her into trouble.

Behind the Mask

These seven characters each struggled with relationships in their own way, and in every case their personal struggles were never recognized as being characteristic of autism.

Social relationships, whether with friends, family, coworkers, or romantic partners, are challenging for autistic women. The struggle begins in early childhood and continues to adulthood but is often unnoticed or misidentified. Because many people who are not autistic also have trouble with relationships, here are some things to take into consideration.

➤ As a girl, did she keep to herself during recess, perhaps walking around the perimeter of the playground, or reading a book, or engaging in solitary or sensory-focused play? Perhaps she often asked to stay in the classroom or go to the library to avoid going out with the other children.

➤ In new, unfamiliar social situations, does she tend to freeze up and watch others to see how to behave, imitating them when she can?

➤ Was it a mystery to her how the other children made friends so easily, while friendship always seems to be out of her grasp?

➤ Did she allow herself to be used by mean girls, to do their bidding and put up with their insults, just so she could be part of a group of friends?

➤ Does she feel as if everyone else got a secret how-to handbook on how to make friends, but she didn't get hers?

➤ Does she tend towards extremes, either fading into the background completely or coming on way too strong?

➤ Is she taken by surprise when a friend gets mad at her or when a romance goes sour, and does she let the relationship end without ever knowing what went wrong?

➤ Is she naive in relationships and therefore vulnerable and easily taken advantage of?

➤ Is she much more interested in people who are older or younger than she is, such as hanging out with the moms during sleepovers as a child, or as a teen or adult, volunteering to watch the children when families get together?

➤ At a party, would she rather spend time with the host's dog or cat instead of the human guests?

➤ When the other girls played imaginatively with their fashion dolls, getting them dressed up to go on dates, did she watch from the sidelines, pretending to care? Did she try to direct them to follow her script? Did she focus on organizing the dresses and accessories, or just do her own thing and leave them alone?

➤ When other girls acted out pretend play, such as playing house and pretending to be the mother, or pretending to be superheroes, was she uninterested, or confused, or disdainful, because clearly they are children and are neither a mother nor a superhero?

➤ Does she have a persona, or alter ego, or character that she pretends to be when meeting new people, dating, or participating in a job interview, to give herself confidence?

In Her Own Words

"I have always tried to figure out what part, what persona, I will play in social situations or groups. I tend to gravitate toward being the 'nice and funny' one. Making people laugh is a good way to know that you are doing something right. The response is obvious: people are enjoying your company, at least a little, if they laugh at your jokes. If I strive to be nice and funny, then I know my place in the social circle."

— *Denise S.*

PART II
REPETITIVE PATTERNS

"Restricted, repetitive patterns of behavior, interests, or activities..."

— *Diagnostic and Statistical Manual for Mental Disorders, Fifth Edition (DSM-5)*

"Interestingly, one of the findings from research into sex differences in children with autism was that girls with autism do not have the same stereotypical, rigid interests as boys (Carter et al, 2007). My research certainly found that repetitive and restricted behaviours were completely the norm for the girls studied but that topic type differed."

— *Sarah Hendricks, autistic author*

Chapter Four

STEREOTYPED BEHAVIORS

If You're Happy and You Know It, Flap Your Hands

"Stereotyped or repetitive motor movements, use of objects, or speech ..."

— *Diagnostic and Statistical Manual for Mental Disorders, Fifth Edition (DSM-5)*

"One thing I loved about being in the theatre was the warm ups. The whole cast and crew would stand in a circle, shake out their hands, arms, and bodies, and do vocal exercises like lip trills, tongue twisters, or just practicing enunciating clear consonants by repeating nonsense syllables like 'Buh-duh-guh' or 'tuh-pah-kuh-ta'. When everybody has to stim, it's just normal."

— *Cat*

Stereotyped behaviors, or self-stimulatory behaviors, are repetitive body movements that do not appear to serve an obvious social function. The function is usually assumed to be automatic reinforcement: things people do simply because they enjoy doing them, not necessarily because they serve any purpose.

In fact, though, many self-stimulatory behaviors, or "stims," do serve a purpose. They can indicate that a person is struggling with a situation and needs help. They may be used to help self-regulate stress or sensory overload. Stims can express joy and excitement when there are no words sufficient to the task. Or, people may engage in stims just for the pleasure of it. If you've never tried flapping your hands, try it the next time you're feeling tense. It does feel good, doesn't it?

Since stims in general don't harm anybody and since they often serve a purpose even if we cannot see the purpose, we should not try to stop someone from moving their body in ways that feel right to them. The same goes for mannerisms involving moving objects, and verbal or vocal stims. If no one is hurt, then don't try to stop the behavior just because people might be uncomfortable with it. Forcing a person to stop doing a thing that is a useful stress reliever for them may lead to other stims which may not be so benign, such as self-harm, biting their hands, slapping their faces, and banging their heads. It would be better for the rest of the world to get comfortable with the fact that some people enjoy moving their hands, fingers, bodies, or objects, or using their voices in ways that are different from what others consider the "norm." Let's look a little more closely at what motor, object, and speech stims might look like in girls and women.

A motor stim is a movement or body posture. This includes small, subtle behaviors like tapping fingers, flaring nostrils, bouncing a foot or knee, wringing hands, pulling or twisting fingers, or rubbing the palms repetitively on upper arms or thighs. It can be more obvious, such as flapping hands, waving arms, or holding the arms or body in an unusual posture. Whole body movements include rocking side to side or back and forth, either while sitting or standing. It may show up as spinning around in a circle with arms out or spinning around on an office chair. Other movements include bouncing or jumping, pacing, walking on tiptoe, or marching in place. People often find these activities to be cute when girls exhibit them. When she spins they say she is dancing, when she flaps she's pretending to be a bird, and when she flutters her fingers they say she's playing an invisible piano. In early childhood these movements are dismissed, and for girls who are smart enough to notice their differences, they learn to mask their mannerisms at a young age and save their stims until they're alone.

Object stims, or repetitive use of objects, may include many things. A toddler may have a ritual of picking up a block from the floor at her left side, turning it over once in her hands, and then placing it down to her right side. She can spend hours like this, as long as someone keeps moving the pile of blocks from her right back to her left side. Another little girl lines up every DVD in the house in one long line across the floor, becoming upset if anyone tries to move one of them. When she gets older, she's the child who lines up her crayons on her desk and the adult whose bookshelf is perfectly organized by size and color. A child might repetitively throw every small object the moment they get their hands on it, and later learn to throw only balls or crumpled up paper. Some girls must carry around a specific object with them wherever they go. We're not talking about a blanky or doll or stuffed animal here, but something unusual, with no obvious rhyme or reason to her choice. As an adult, she may choose something small enough to fit into her purse or pocket, so no one knows about it.

Vocal stims can take several forms. Repetition of words, phrases, or sentences is called echolalia. This may be present in otherwise non- or pre-verbal children as well as those with other meaningful speech. One girl may repeat verbatim the last few words that someone said to her. Adults ask, "Do you want an apple?" and when the girl repeats, "want an apple," they give her one and are surprised when she throws or bats it away. Another girl may repeat complete sentences or conversations she has heard in the past, or parts of movies or television shows. A child who says, "Cheese, cheese, cheese," may be hungry, asking for a piece of cheese. She may want to go to Chuck E. Cheese or order pizza. Possibly she may want to watch *Jeeves & Wooster* on DVD but can't pronounce "Jeeves." She may see a camera in the room, and her response to a camera is to say "Cheese." It's difficult to know what a child means when they repeat a word or sound over and over. Echolalia may seem meaningless, but there is often intention behind the repeated words. If a girl repeats a line from her favorite movie, perhaps it somehow relates to the present situation. She wants to comment but lacks the language to come up with her own statement, so she borrows one from TV. It is also possible that she is repeating, "Linoleum, linoleum, linoleum," simply because it's fun to say. Try it. The sheer enjoyment of creating and repeating a string of interesting sounds can be reinforcing in and of itself.

For many girls and women, the repetitive movements, use of objects, or speech can be subtle. As they get older and realize their behaviors are seen as odd, they often try to hide what they're doing, or they only engage in these pursuits when they are alone. It's all too easy to miss these autistic characteristics when women have been masking them their whole lives. Read on to see how each of our fictional female figures demonstrated these behaviors and how the behaviors were missed as they grew up.

Fictional Female Figures

CHEYENNE

Motor Mannerisms

No one knew about Cheyenne's secret repetitive movements. When riding in a car, looking out at the scenery they passed, she would flare her nostrils each time they passed a tree. Each time they passed a curb cut or driveway, she blinked, and when they passed over a railroad track, she curled her toes. No one saw her doing this. As an adult, when a counselor asked her about any unusual behaviors, Cheyenne didn't tell her. It had seemed so natural for so many years, and she did it in a subtle way. Still, the idea of describing this ritual out loud seemed weird, and she couldn't bring herself to admit to it.

Use of Objects

When she was a girl, Cheyenne was given a set of construction blocks that fit together to create buildings or vehicles. It also included tiny people with yellow cylindrical heads and body parts you could mix and match. She put a female head on a superhero body and created her own character that she named BraveAnne. BraveAnne wasn't afraid of anything, and she always spoke her mind. Cheyenne started carrying BraveAnne in her pocket wherever she went. When she felt shy and afraid, she put her hand in her pocket and held BraveAnne, and she felt stronger. She never stopped carrying the toy, even after she grew up and got married. When her husband came across it in one of her pockets while doing the laundry, she felt ashamed at first and then tried to explain. Gabe got it, and he surprised her on her birthday with a framed picture he had created of Cheyenne as BraveAnne. It was her most treasured possession for the rest of her life.

Vocal Stims

Cheyenne's vocal stim was subtle, and most people didn't even notice it. She had a phrase she whispered to herself whenever she felt stressed or overwhelmed: "Issoay. Issoay. Eryingilleeoay." This was her private way of saying, "It's okay. It's okay. Everything will be okay." Usually she pronounced the "Issoay. Issoay." on an inhalation, breathing it in, and then whispering "Eryingilleeoay" on an exhalation. This allowed her to keep repeating it without pause for as long as necessary until she felt more in control. No one could see her lips moving, and no one was close enough to hear her whisper. Once, when her friend Bethany fell down and scraped her knee badly, Cheyenne became flustered, feeling her friend's pain intensely. She said out loud, "Issoay. Issoay. Eryingilleeoay," to try to help, but everyone looked at her strangely. She was embarrassed, and from then on she made sure that her verbal ritual was completely undetectable by others.

PENELOPE

Motor Mannerisms

Penelope had a motor mannerism of repetitive fingerspelling. She had learned the finger alphabet when Peter was taught sign language as a potential way to increase his communication skills as a child. Now, when standing in a line, or anytime she was not otherwise engaged and her hands were empty, her fingers were constantly flying, although her arms were held straight down at her sides, spelling so rapidly that no one could fathom the meaning.

Use of Objects

Three objects which were never far from Penelope were a tiny piece of dinosaur bone, a small porcelain egg, and a fragment of amber. She had them drilled and strung onto a necklace so she could always wear them, hidden beneath her buttoned-up shirt. They reminded her of her passions and of her love for Peter, who shared these interests with her.

Vocal Stims

Approximately once every five to fifteen seconds, Penelope emitted a short, dry cough. This was not brought on by a cold or allergy but was a constant background to her day. Students secretly kept data and placed bets on how many times she would cough during a lecture. Penelope was not even aware that she was engaging in a vocal stim; it was so natural to her that it didn't even register.

AKIKO

Motor Mannerisms

When Akiko was a toddler, she tiptoed everywhere she went. Her heels never seemed to touch the ground. The pediatrician said this was normal at her age, so her parents never questioned it, even though it continued for many years. She loved to stand on top of the coffee table on her toes, rapidly shifting her weight from the right to the left toe as if dancing, while holding her favorite objects up to examine them against the light. When she got older, she walked with her hands clasped in front of her chest rather than swinging them by her sides. In school, when she was overwhelmed by sensory experiences, she held her hands fisted facing outward at shoulder height and rapidly shook them, as if they were vibrating. Her teachers had heard that autistic people flapped their open hands, so her stim did not raise concerns. No one thought her behaviors were particularly autistic, just odd.

50

Use of Objects

Straws always fascinated Akiko. She loved to push the end of one straw into the opening of another straw to make it twice as long, and when she got frustrated in the attempts, her parents helped her construct long sticks which were four or five straws long. While on tiptoe on the coffee table, she raised the straws above her head and smiled while staring at them. She held them between her thumb and fingertip and let them tip back and forth, finding the perfect balance. Balance was important. When she went on to find more and more things she could stick together to make longer and longer sticks, her parents started buying her tube toys that she would put together with wooden spoons and sticks she found on the ground, anything long and thin.

Vocal Stims

Akiko's verbal stims were the repetitive sounds she made, "ff-ff-ff-ff-ff." There were always five brief sounds close together, with a pause and inhalation, and then five more. Her parents supposed it was just an unusual comfort sound she liked to make. When she was under stress, she emitted a louder "VV-VV-VV-VV-VV!" They learned to check and see what was wrong whenever they heard that sound. As she got older and started school, she substituted a subtler mannerism of tapping her teeth to her lower lip five times in quick succession, hoping no one noticed. When she was upset or overwhelmed by heightened sensory situations, she bit her lip until it bled.

RUTH

Motor Mannerisms

Ruth was a rocker. Before falling asleep as an infant, lying on her tummy with her knees tucked under her, she rocked herself to sleep with the whole crib rocking along with her. She tended to rock forward and backward whenever she was seated, and the speed of her rocking increased along with her anxiety. When she was agitated, she bent forward until her chest almost touched her lap with each rock. Standing, she rocked from side to side, shifting her weight from one foot to the other. As an adult, she loves rocking chairs, hoping that her rocking will seem more natural to others.

Use of Objects

There were a number of "lucky" or "magical" objects Ruth collected. A special rock, the slip of paper in a fortune cookie, a square plastic tag from the wrapper on a loaf of bread, anything was fair game to end up in her pocket. She ascribed mysterious powers to each one in her imagination. She could never explain to anyone else why she simply had to keep that particular bit of what they called trash, so she kept her special things secret.

Vocal Stims

Not all vocal stims stand out. Ruth has a few things she repeats again and again, which help her maintain her composure when her anxiety starts looming large. She repeats, "Okay, okay, okay, okay," and "Let it go, let it go, let it go, let it go," always in groups of four. Because the words themselves are not especially unusual, no one recognizes this as a verbal mannerism, but this is what it is to her.

OLIVIA

Motor Mannerisms

Olivia used to love to spin herself around, again and again, until she got dizzy and fell down. If she saw a swiveling desk chair, she felt compelled to sit on it and spin, which got her in trouble when it was the teacher's chair she took over. Any time she passed a tetherball pole that no one was using, she held it with her right hand and walked around and around the pole. Spinning or walking in circles was never boring for her, as she lost herself in the pleasing repetitive movement.

Use of Objects

As a girl, Olivia used to line up her blocks on the floor, going all the way out the door, down the hall, and into the living room, until she ran out of blocks. If someone rearranged two blocks while she wasn't looking, she would find and correct the mistake. When her parents tried to clean them up, she cried as if her heart would break. In school, she lined all twelve of her pencils up before she could begin any task. As an adult, she had her books arranged just so on the shelves and her kitchen utensils hanging from hooks in order of size. If someone asked her why, she said she just liked things to be organized a certain way. She couldn't explain to them that the books would be sad if they were not next to their family of books that all had the same number of words in the title. People wouldn't understand that the kitchen utensils had invisible lines extending from them and that the lines would get tangled if she didn't arrange them correctly. These explanations sounded illogical even to her, so she never shared them. Outwardly, she seemed like a typical hyper-organizer with obsessive-compulsive disorder, and autism was not suspected.

Vocal Stims

Olivia could repeat lines, songs, and entire scenes from her favorite cartoons, musicals, and animated movies. She imitated the tone of voice of each character, every inflection exactly as it was in the movie. When she felt an overwhelming urge to run away and escape a stressful situation, she imagined she was an ice princess and sang about letting it go. When she felt especially joyful, she sang a song from another movie about how awesome everything is. Her parents learned to sense her moods and needs from the lines and songs she repeated. They were proud of her exceptional memory, and it didn't occur to them that this could also be a characteristic of autism.

TIFFANY

Motor Mannerisms

What some might call "rapid blinking" on Tiffany looked like fluttering her eyelashes. When she bit the insides of her mouth until they bled, she looked to the world like she was gently pursing her lips in an adorable way. Several times a day, she locked herself in a bathroom and shook her hands wildly, rocking back and forth almost violently until she could find her calm place again. Eventually she was able to return to the set with abject apologies for making everyone wait for her. The cast and crew assumed she must have irritable bowel syndrome, so no one ever questioned her frequent bathroom breaks. These times of solitude, when she could move her body in whatever weird way felt right to her at the moment, kept Tiffany sane.

Use of Objects

Pebbles, rocks, stones, even bits of gravel—all were wonderful to Tiffany, and having one in her pocket at all times gave her peace.

Vocal Stims

Quiet humming was Tiffany's go-to vocal stim, although she was not even aware that she was doing it. People she worked with thought it was either charming or annoying but for the most part ignored it as an affectation. Her parents and Danny could judge her level of stress by her humming and call for a break before she became overwhelmed.

HEIDI

Motor Mannerisms

Heidi loved to jump up and down. She didn't even need trampolines to keep bouncing (although she loved them). If she was happy or excited, she bobbed up and down while flapping her hands, and her parents called her "Birdie" as if she were trying to fly. When she was frustrated, she stomped her feet firmly on the floor. Any time she could climb up somewhere high and jump off it, she was in heaven. Although bouncing and flapping in boys was recognized as an autistic trait, in Heidi no one thought of autism. They just thought she was an active, happy little girl.

Use of Objects

When she was two years old, Heidi found a gallon jug of fabric softener in the laundry room. She dragged it out and carried it with her all day. Every time her mother tried to put it away, she screamed at top volume, and her mother relented. When Heidi finally fell asleep, her mother took the jug and put it on the highest shelf in the laundry room. The next day she found Heidi dragging it around again. Her attachment to this bottle was intense, and her parents worried about it. Even though it was unlikely that Heidi would be able to open the child-proof lid, while she was asleep one night they poured all of the liquid into another container which they hid in the garage. Heidi picked it up in the morning, lifted it, and then fell to the floor sobbing. She could not be consoled. They tried putting a gallon of water into the jug so it would be the same weight, but Heidi shook it and rejected it again, in tears. Apparently the way the thicker liquid sloshed inside was different from the water, and it was unacceptable. After agonizing over this weird new behavior, her parents eventually gave in and let her have a full jug of her own, with the lid secured with several layers of duct tape. This seemed to placate Heidi, and she continued to carry the jug from room to room and even bring it in the car with her for over a year. Later, Heidi kept extra books in her backpack and carried it everywhere, loving the feel of the weight on her shoulders. Her parents never told her about the time in her life when her favorite object was a jug of fabric softener, because they were ashamed of how weird it was and relieved when she finally forgot about it. When a psychologist asked if she had any unusual objects she had to carry around as a child, Heidi said no, because she had no memory of it and her parents had kept the secret.

Vocal Stims

Every week Heidi had new favorite words that she loved to sing out at top volume. Throughout the day her parents would hear her joyfully crying, "Panda, panda, panda!" or "Novemmmmber!" Their least favorite was the week she discovered the word 'diarrhea.' Her parents agreed early on that they would refrain from ever using any curse words in her presence, for as they said, "An expletive un-deleted is an expletive repeated." Heidi didn't remember repeating words during her childhood, and they never thought to mention it.

Behind the Mask

Every one of these seven girls exhibited motor mannerisms, unusual use of objects, and verbal or vocal stims. For each, the behaviors began in early childhood, and many continued to adulthood in some form. Often these mannerisms are masked, or they are supplanted by a more subtle behavior that they taught themselves in an effort to fit in with others. Their repetitive behaviors were missed, and their autism continued to be unrecognized.

An action, a way of manipulating things, or a repetitive verbal behavior may be subtle, or even invisible. It may be made small so as to escape notice or be reserved for alone time when no one can comment, question, or judge the behavior. It is important to develop a relationship of trust so they feel comfortable sharing their awkward or unexpected behaviors with you. Only by asking questions that reveal these behaviors can answers be known. Here are some examples:

➢ When you're overwhelmed, are there ways you move your body, like rocking or pacing, that help you self-regulate or express that feeling?

➢ Are there subtle things you do at these times that others don't notice, like squeezing your arms or clenching your jaw?

➢ When you're excited and overjoyed, are there ways you move your body to express that joy, like bouncing or doing "jazz hands?"

➢ Have you noticed that people thought the ways you moved were unusual, so you trained yourself to stop or tone down those movements?

➢ Have you had favorite objects that other people may have thought were odd, or collections of things other people would never think to collect?

➢ Have you found more pleasure in arranging and organizing things like toys, utensils, books, or office supplies, than you do in actually using them?

➢ Do you have a special feeling for certain favorite numbers, letters, colors, shapes, or other things that are difficult to explain?

➢ Have you enjoyed repeating words or sounds that are fun to say again and again?

➢ Have you enjoyed making up words or creating new languages?

➢ Do people ever think you are talking in another accent or using words or phrases that are unexpected or old-fashioned?

In Her Own Words

"When I was in school I used to stim all the time. My teachers constantly told me I wasn't allowed to rock back and forth, clap, or click my pen as I was 'too distracting.' So I started using fidget toys that were small and easy to hide. Then my school put a ban on all fidget toys as they were also 'too distracting.' I tried telling them it helps me focus, but no one listened to me. They told me I was just being dramatic and was looking for attention. When I was no longer allowed to do any stimming movements and couldn't play with fidget toys, I spent all day at school trying to be 'normal.' I was so angry that I wasn't allowed to be myself, it took a huge toll on my mental health. I started to think that I was the problem."

— *Molly*

Chapter Five

RIGIDITY

If It's Worth Doing, It's Worth Doing the Same Way Every Time

"Insistence on sameness, inflexible adherence to routines, or ritualized patterns of verbal or nonverbal behavior..."

> — *Diagnostic and Statistical Manual for Mental Disorders, Fifth Edition (DSM-5)*

"Neurotypical people seem to think and feel that it's okay to be rigid as long as their ideas are shared by enough people."

> — *Dr. Temple Grandin, autistic author, speaker, professor*

M any people have a routine they are comfortable with and prefer the familiar to the adventurous. For our autistic girls and women, this goes beyond a preference to a need. When the world seems chaotic, they struggle to hold on to the routines they are used to, and the rituals they create, to help them manage their stress. Having something new thrown at them out of left field can stop them in their tracks. It could lead to a total meltdown, dissolving into uncontrollable tears, or to a shutdown, even becoming catatonic and unable to move or talk.

It may be a ritual that they have created for themselves, such as a special way of making coffee or brushing their teeth. It could be a routine that has been imposed on them, such as a school or work schedule, but which they have embraced. In either case, having to move outside of their comfort zone and away from their familiar, structured life can be exceptionally difficult and exhausting.

As young children, many autistic girls have a vivid and specific memory of how something happened the first time and a strong expectation or need for it to happen the same way every time. If their mother walked into the kindergarten class and sat with them for five minutes on the first day of school, their idea of what happens in kindergarten includes their mother sitting with them for five minutes every single day of the year. Trying to change that expectation results in much greater and longer-lasting distress than a typical kindergartner, who misses their mother at first and then gets interested in the other children, toys, and activities, might feel. It would have been better for our autistic girl if they could have made a special visit to get used to the room and meet the teacher with their mother before the first day of school so that it would be familiar. Then, on the first day, their mother could leave them at the door as the other parents do, setting the stage for how every day of kindergarten will begin.

For most of us, a detour on the way to work is a mild annoyance because it may make us late, but it is soon forgotten. For an autistic woman, having to take a different route to work can ruin her whole day, making it difficult for her to cope with the many other stressors in her life.

Many people would love it if someone threw them a surprise party, but do not attempt to surprise an autistic girl or woman with this kind of unexpected event. It will not be appreciated in the spirit of friendship that it was offered with. She will have to deal with not one surprise, but multiple stressful events. First, if she was told that something else would happen, such as lunch alone with a friend, and then found out that instead it would be a party with many friends, this would be a difficult adjustment. Her expectation of a one-on-one lunch would be ripped away unexpectedly. Second, the sensory aspect of the surprise itself is traumatic, walking into a darkened room and having a bunch of people jump up and yell. This can be terrifying, even if the words they are yelling are "Surprise! Happy birthday!" Extreme stress can result in a sudden decrease in the ability to understand and use spoken language for many autists, so the words may not register as strongly as the reality of people jumping out of the darkness yelling. Finally, she must live with the knowledge that when her friends tried so hard to do something nice for her, she was ungrateful and could not enjoy it, even to make them happy. There is a lot of self-blame after events like this, reliving the moment in memory and being ashamed and appalled at her own response all over again. Read on to see the role that rigidity plays in the lives of our fictional female figures.

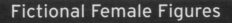
Fictional Female Figures

CHEYENNE

Familiar routines gave great comfort to Cheyenne, and any time she had to deviate from her predictable schedule, it was extremely stressful for her. When she was a newborn, she had diaper rashes, and her pediatrician recommended changing her diaper as soon as she woke up, before feeding her. It was effective, and by two months of age she no longer had any diaper rash. Her mother started trying to feed her before changing her diaper since she would have to change it after the feeding anyway, but Cheyenne resisted strongly. She cried and turned away every time her mother tried to feed her first, even if she was hungry and had a dry diaper. They had to continue in the same way they had started, changing before feeding, at her insistence. It was easier to do things the way Cheyenne wanted. They didn't always understand why things had to be done in a particular way or order, but they accepted it.

Starting in elementary school and continuing throughout her lifetime, Cheyenne had a very particular morning ritual. Her toothbrush, toothpaste, cup, hairbrush and towel all had to be laid out in a very specific order before she began her routine. She adjusted each item a few times before she felt comfortable enough to start getting ready for the day. Her parents had learned not to interrupt her during this process. If they called to her to hurry up or to ask what she wanted for lunch, she froze. She remained perfectly motionless for a minute or two, and once she came out of her shutdown, she shook herself and started over. It didn't matter that she had already brushed her teeth; the entire routine had to begin again from the first step.

As an adult, Cheyenne still had many things she had to have happen in a specific way. On their first real date, Gabe got lost trying to find the restaurant, and they ended up driving all the way around a small lake before they found it. From then on, every time they went back to that restaurant she insisted on going the same way. Fortunately, Gabe was happy to go along with whatever made Cheyenne happy.

PENELOPE

There was no question that Penelope was persnickety. Everything had to be just so in her life. If the white board in her lecture hall was stained by permanent marker, she demanded that it be replaced, even if the mark was small and in a corner.

She was rigid about language and labels, too. When meeting someone new, if they asked, "May I call you Penny, or do you prefer Penelope?" her response was that they should call her Dr. Potter. If a student referred to a colleague as "Professor," she was quick to point out that the person was not a professor, but only an associate professor, or an assistant professor, or, worst of all, an adjunct instructor. Full professorship was something she had achieved after years of hard work and research, and she did not take kindly to others being granted the same title out of sheer sloppiness of speech. Everything and every position had a name. It was respectful and proper to use the correct name and to tell others when they had used the language incorrectly. It never occurred to Penelope that if she made these corrections in front of a class, or especially in front of the colleague who had been so mislabeled, people would find it offensive. How could the truth be offensive? If he wanted to be called Professor, let him put in the years, do the research, and publish rather than perish as an adjunct. People's feelings meant very little to Penelope, except when it came to her brother. His feelings and his well-being were more important to her than her own.

AKIKO

Akiko was rigid in many ways since early infancy. When she wanted something, she tried to communicate but often ended up in tears. Her parents learned that when they found the perfect blanket or stuffed toy that she preferred, they should buy as many as they could. It was a nightmare trying to introduce a close but not identical substitute when the original got lost or worn out. When they found clothes she was comfortable in, they purchased every size she would grow into so she could continue to wear her familiar favorites. It had always been difficult for Akiko to adjust to any new situation, a new home, a new job, and especially people. It took her weeks to get used to a new classmate, coworker, or neighbor. She couldn't explain her reasoning to anyone else. If she told people that she had to see a new person exactly seven times before she could greet them, they would think she was weird. It was better to be seen as rude than as weird.

RUTH

Ruth insisted on everything being the same. Throughout her childhood, every breakfast was served on a blue plate, every lunch on a red plate, and every dinner on a green plate. It seemed unusual, and her mother worried that she was a bad parent, spoiling Ruth rather than teaching her to accept any color plate. After several missed meals, though, her mother went along out of concern for her nutrition. If the proper color of plate were dirty, her mother hand-washed it specially for Ruth, knowing she would never accept a different color.

Ruth needed the blinds in the living room to be at the same height and had to have everything in even numbers, never odd. Symmetry was important to her. When her teacher taught them sign language, Ruth refused to do certain signs because her two hands would be in different positions. She never held hands in a circle during Scouts because she hated the feeling of two different palms, different sizes, textures, temperatures, levels of dampness. She just crossed her arms and opted out. At bedtime, her parents learned to kiss her goodnight in the center of her forehead rather than on one cheek, which would require the same pressure of kiss on the opposite cheek. If her dad patted her knee, she surreptitiously patted her other knee the same number of times. Later, when a psychologist asked about early behaviors, her parents never mentioned any of these things because they didn't seem important and they found such things embarrassing. The signs were not obvious because she learned to engage in them subtly, so Ruth's autism continued to be unrecognized.

OLIVIA

Olivia's parents were puzzled by her inflexibility. As a child, when her dad said she could have four small cookies, she was quite adamant that she could not possibly eat four and begged for five. Her dad thought she was trying to get more than her share, and he stood his ground. Finally, Olivia admitted defeat and sadly asked for three cookies instead of four. This was her parents' first clue that their little girl had ideas that they might not understand but that she felt strongly about. She would not or could not be flexible about those things that were important to her.

In elementary school, Olivia had a full meltdown, crumpled in tears on the floor, when she walked into her class and saw a substitute teacher. After that, her parents kept her home when they knew in advance there would be a sub.

Even as an adult, she continued to be inflexible and particular in her ways. Friends and family members who went to restaurants with Olivia learned that it was best to just let her choose the restaurant, the booth, and her seat at the table. They assumed this was her OCD, but it also fit the criterion for autistic rigidity.

TIFFANY

Even after she was a legal adult, able to make all of her own decisions, Tiffany's parents intervened on her behalf, and to her great relief. They made sure that her call time was always the same, no matter what show she was on. The producers thought they were being pushy parents just trying to prove they had clout, but her parents knew the truth. Tiffany would have a terrible day if it started even five minutes before or after the expected time. She could not "roll with" schedule changes, not because she was a spoiled prima donna, but because she was autistic, although unrecognized.

Her autism was also why she had so much trouble with idioms and parts of speech: she was a very literal thinker. After an especially long and exhausting day on the set, the director told her she could go and hit the sack. She smiled and nodded, but inside she was in a quandary. What sack was she supposed to hit? How hard should she hit it, and why? She didn't remember anything about a sack in the stage directions in her script. Would someone demonstrate the action required so that she could imitate it? She was good at that.

Before she could ask for a demo to mimic "hitting the sack," her mother took her by the arm and led her to the waiting car. What a relief to be going home at last. She fell asleep in the car, completely exhausted just from being around people all day.

HEIDI

Heidi had rituals that she had to go through. As a small child, every time she washed her hands, she clapped them in the stream of running water exactly three times, once per second, and then shrieked in delight for three seconds. Clap, shriek, repeat. Her parents were always telling her not to be so splashy and noisy, and they never realized that this was not random loud water play, but a very specific repeated ritual.

Heidi loved everything about her job with the post office. The first time she was assigned a right-hand drive mail truck, she was ecstatic. "Wot, are we British?" she said in an exaggerated accent. A few of her colleagues chuckled, so she repeated the joke every day. The laughs came fewer and farther between, until Heidi realized people were annoyed. She kept her silence each morning when she picked up her vehicle, but once she was a block away she shouted it joyfully at the top of her voice: "Wot, are we British?" As long as she was inside the vehicle, she spoke in an English accent, but as soon as both feet were on the ground, she spoke in her usual voice. This ritual was important to her, and it brought her joy even when she kept it to herself.

 Behind the Mask

Unusual rigidity was present for each of these seven girls, and they shared a need for routine, or insistence on sameness. And yet, because of the small, quiet way most of these behaviors manifested, autism was not suspected.

Here are some questions that may help you to uncover autistic characteristics related to rigidity and a strong need for routine, even when they have been hidden well:

➢ When there was a substitute teacher, was it usually harder for you to cope with than it was for the others in your class?

➢ Were family vacations difficult for you and not much fun, because everything was so different and unpredictable?

➢ If someone were to throw you a surprise party, what would that be like for you?

➢ If there is a detour on your way to work, can it throw off your whole day?

➢ What would you do if friends propose a spur-of-the moment trip to the mall?

➢ If you had a doctor's appointment for a regular check-up, and once you got there you learned that you must also have a blood draw, would it be extremely difficult for you to adjust your expectations and be okay letting them draw your blood?

➢ Does it take you longer than most people to get used to a new home or a new office or a new coworker?

➢ When you expected to eat a certain meal but it was unexpectedly unavailable, was it so distressing that you ended up going hungry rather than making a different food choice?

71

➢ If you plan to spend an evening alone watching something on television, and a good friend or much-loved family member drops by, is it nearly impossible for you to enjoy their company because you did not expect them?

➢ Do you have scripts in mind for how to greet people at work or respond to specific situations requiring a verbal response?

➢ Do you like to eat the same foods every day and would have trouble thinking of what to eat if you couldn't follow that routine?

➢ Are there little things you do that people don't notice, and if you had to explain why you did them no one would understand and would think you were strange?

➢ Do you have special ways of doing things in the same way every time, and if you get interrupted in the middle of your routine, do you have to start over or shut down completely?

In Her Own Words

"I don't handle transitions or changes well, especially when they're not planned far in advance. Even when things are planned out, if it's a change to my daily routine, I still struggle with it. It feels like an emotional reaction and I get anxious. I try to figure out logically why I react this way, but most of the time I don't know why. Others can just roll with things, but I can't. The people closest to me understand that sometimes I can't do something.

With others, though, I have to come up with an appropriate excuse for why I can't attend something or participate in something, or they'll think I'm weird."

— *Kara, autistic woman, diagnosed at age 44*

Chapter Six

INTERESTS

If You Love Something, Never Let it Go

"Highly restricted, fixated interests that are abnormal in intensity or focus ..."
— *Diagnostic and Statistical Manual for Mental Disorders, Fifth Edition (DSM-5)*

"Many interests enjoyed by women with autism can appear as fairly common... but ... the depth of knowledge and the diligence put into the learning is way in excess of a 'hobby.'"

— *Sarah Hendrickx, autistic author*

We all have interests, things we enjoy doing or learning about. We love to talk about our interests sometimes, especially when we find someone who likes the same things we do. But, with autistic people, their interests may be seen by others as unusual in two ways.

First, an interest may be considered unusual in intensity. Our autistic girls may love horses, which seems right in step with many other little girls who also love horses. What distinguishes our girl here is that her interest is much more deeply felt and extensively researched. Many girls love to imagine the horse they would like to own, what color it would be, what they would name it. Our girl on the spectrum, though, may be the only one who has memorized all of the breeds of horses and can trace their evolution from the earliest eohippus. She can name every equine body part, poll to pastern and crest to fetlock, and is surprised when the other horse-loving girls don't understand what she's talking about. Later, when the others forget about horses and move on to makeup, hair styles, and boys, our autistic girl remains faithful to her love of horses, which may become a lifelong devotion. Still, because she was interested in the same thing many girls find interesting, no one considered it to be an "autistic special interest."

The second way that autistic interests may differ from typical interests is their focus. Our girls on the spectrum may have interests that the other girls don't get or that they consider weird. When a young girl is fascinated by umbrella construction, or medieval diseases, or true crime stories, or native plants, it can be difficult to find other girls who share her interest. Luckily, the internet exists, so she can find people she can relate to. In the meantime, she has learned that when she talks about the things she loves, other people look at her strangely or ask her why she would be interested in such things. She can't explain why she loves what she loves, so she learns early to keep her interests to herself and mask her excitement when she thinks about her favorite things. Masking may or may not be conscious as over time it becomes natural to hide her feelings and imitate the other girls' expressions. Masking, pretending to be like everyone else, is a survival skill learned early by many girls. She may not realize that not everyone does this. Over time, though, masking will become more exhausting and difficult.

Let's read on to learn about our fictional female figures and their interests.

 Fictional Female Figures

CHEYENNE

Unusual in Intensity

Most little girls love dolls, but Cheyenne's interest was unusual in its intensity. She deeply loved the Kirsten pioneer girl doll her grandmother had given her. It was part of a collection of dolls from various eras in American history. Each doll had their own story, and there were period clothes and furniture for each one. She loved to set Kirsten up next to her little blue bed and log stool, and hang all of her dresses and aprons on display. She never played with her, but she loved making tableaux, arranging and rearranging all of the little accessories, and reading and re-reading her stories. When Bethany had a doll tea party and invited Cheyenne and a few other girls, Cheyenne was thrilled! She set Kirsten up at the table and started talking excitedly about her doll's origin story, life on the pioneer trail, and how they made their own clothes and candles. She explained what kind of food they ate in Kirsten's day and how different cooking was back then. After a while, she realized that no one else was talking, and the other girls were staring at her as if she had dropped in from another planet. Bethany quickly stepped in to ask if anyone wanted more tea, and the conversation moved on. Cheyenne was mortified that she had gone on and on about her doll when no one else was interested. They only wanted to eat the refreshments and talk about school or TV shows. Cheyenne promised herself that she wouldn't let that happen again. From that day on, whenever she was around a group of girls, she stayed quiet and watched. When the other girls smiled or laughed, she smiled or laughed in the same way. No one ever suspected that she felt like a pretender in a foreign world, more at home on the prairie with Kirsten than she was with girls from her own historical era.

Unusual in Focus

When Cheyenne was very young, her parents showed her the usual fairy tale animated features. Instead of pretending to be a princess, though, her focus was always on the villains. Why were they so bad? Why didn't they help the princess instead of being mean? She couldn't understand why anyone would choose to be a villain when it was so easy to be nice. It troubled her deeply. As soon as she could read, she devoured every murder mystery she could get her hands on. Soon her interest turned from cozy drawing room dramas to tales of true crimes. Serial killers were her favorite, historical and contemporary. She could not get enough of reading, watching documentaries, and listening to podcasts about them. Her parents, Bethany, and later even Gabe were puzzled by sweet Cheyenne's fascination with such a morbid topic, but they couldn't dissuade her from her research. Finally she learned that with some people, it was better to keep this interest private rather than sharing it. As she talked about it less frequently, the people who loved her stopped worrying and gave up trying to change her. They came to realize that her morbid fascination did not mean that she had any murderous inclinations. She simply had an intense desire to try to understand people who were at the core completely different from anyone she knew: humans who behaved inhumanly. As an adult, she found that many women her age also shared this fascination. Her passion for unsolved true crimes and serial killers was no longer unusual in focus, but it was still unusual in intensity.

PENELOPE

Unusual in Intensity

Penelope held three PhDs, in entomology, paleontology, and ornithology. Her interest in entomology began in childhood, when Peter started noticing and becoming fascinated with ants, spiders, and other tiny invertebrates. She learned all she could about them in order to share this interest with him.

The twins were also both interested in dinosaurs from their early years, and she advocated for his teachers to put a dinosaur sticker or stamp on any work paper that they wanted him to finish. It took so little to make

Peter happy; why would anyone begrudge or withhold a dinosaur sticker until after he finished the paper? Let him enjoy it while he worked.

As she worked on her second PhD, she would lecture to him about the different kinds of dinosaurs and everything new she was learning about them. To be sure, she already knew a lot about dinosaurs before she started school, but expanding her knowledge of geology and zoology as she studied vertebrate paleontology was a joy to her, and a joy to share. This interest in dinosaurs led her to ornithology.

Birds are really the closest things to dinosaurs that still exist on our planet, so of course she wanted to learn everything she could about them. On any given weekend, you could spot Penelope and Peter at the zoo, spending hours watching the ostriches or standing on one leg outside the flamingo enclosure. Students or colleagues who happened upon them were astonished at the change in the usually-uptight professor, as they saw her accurately imitate an ostrich's gait and head bob, arms held as wings, to the loud delight of her brother.

As a scholar, Penelope's focuses of interest were not unusual, but the intensity of her interests surpassed even her most specialized colleagues in her fields.

Unusual in Focus

Her intense interest in dinosaurs was the gateway to Penelope's wish to find living dinosaurs to study in person. Cryptozoology became her secret passion, one she knew she could not share with her colleagues without inviting ridicule. In her heart, she believed that it could be possible to find living pterosaurs and other species thought to be extinct. Her private research opened the door to other scientists who felt the same, and she loved reading about their expeditions and interviews with eyewitnesses. Her fondest wish was that one day she and Peter could see a real, live dinosaur in person.

AKIKO

Unusual in Intensity

Akiko loved cats. Of course, many other girls her age also loved cats, but Akiko's passion was over the top. As a toddler she pretended to be a cat most of the time, and her parents were always trying to get her to stop licking her "paw" and wiping her face with it. Every stuffed animal she owned was a cat of some kind, from tiny realistic kittens to a nearly-life-sized tiger. While riding in the car with her parents, whenever they passed by a cat in a yard she would shriek, "Cat!" and beg to stop and pet it. As she got older, she realized they would never pull over to let her pet stray cats, so instead of asking, she described the cat she saw in detail. This was more for her own benefit, to hear herself talking about the cat; she didn't really care if her parents acknowledged her running cat commentary. She knew every breed and its history, and which cat breed had won Cat Fancier's Best in Show every year since she was five. They always had two cats in their household, partly so they could keep each other company, but mostly because her parents worried about how upset she would become when a beloved pet eventually succumbed to old age. There had to be another cat there to comfort their distraught daughter when the inevitable happened. The first time Akiko heard that someone was a "cat person," she was ecstatic, imagining a human-feline mutation. She was disappointed to learn that a "cat person" was just someone who liked cats, not a person who was a cat. When she learned that a "Cat Lady" is a woman who has lots and lots of cats, she knew immediately that was what she wanted to be when she grew up. To take care of all the stray cats that needed homes was the highest moral calling she could aspire to.

Unusual in Focus

Along with her interest in cats, Akiko had many other intense interests that morphed and changed over the course of her lifetime, and many of them were unusual in focus. Because she loved to touch soft fabrics, she became interested in textiles. This led to an interest in silk, and the life and history of silkworms. Her third grade teacher brought in silkworms and mulberry leaves so the class could watch them grow, spin cocoons, and emerge as silkworm moths. All of the children loved this unit, Akiko most of all. She researched online and in the library to find out everything she could about them. It was a shock to learn that in order to make silk thread, the silkworms had to be killed in the cocoons. Otherwise they would emerge as moths, biting their way through the valuable thread. This distressed her so much that she vowed to never wear silk, ever. Learning about silk, though, led her to become interested in Japanese culture, food, history, poetry. This led to her intense interest in Japanese manga and anime. She read through many manga series, rereading them when she ran out of issues, but her absolute favorite was *Chi's Sweet Home*, about a kitten who finds a family. Her favorite anime to watch was *A Whisker Away*, about a girl who can transform herself into a cat. Akiko wished she could do that, and she loved watching and re-watching this favorite any time she felt down and needed to feel better. Many people assumed her strong interest in Japan was related to her family culture, but for Akiko, it had all started with a silkworm.

RUTH

Unusual in Intensity

Lots of little girls love princess movies, including Ruth. Every single one. She watched them again and again, singing and reciting every word along with the movie. Every Halloween she would choose a different princess to be. She learned the origin stories, the old tales of the Grimm brothers and Charles Perrault and Hans Christian Andersen. When she met another little girl who shared her love of princesses, she immediately began discussing the differences between the original folk stories and the modern animated movies. No one was interested, though, and the other girls thought she was strange for even knowing such things. They shared her interest in princess stories, but they did not approach her level of intensity in this shared interest.

Unusual in Focus

As a professional-level worrier, Ruth was an expert on knowing what to worry about (most things) and what not to worry about (not much.) After watching *The Wizard of Oz*, she became fascinated with tornadoes. She believed that knowledge is power, and if she could identify early warning signals in the way the sky looked, she could potentially warn everyone of an approaching tornado and save many lives. She was not comforted in the knowledge that there hadn't been a tornado in her city since before she was born, and even then it had been considered an anomaly. Over the years she progressed from studying tornadoes to weather in general, and then earthquakes, forest fires, and tsunamis. Natural disasters were her passion, and learning about them helped her feel in control. Over the years she branched out beyond natural disasters to immerse herself in learning about the Titanic, the Hindenburg, and 9/11. Other people didn't get why she was so interested in such things, but she was undeterred in her thirst for knowledge on disasters.

OLIVIA

Unusual in Intensity

Olivia was obsessed with a book series about a boy who discovered he was a wizard. She read and re-read every book as soon as it came out, even begging her parents to take her to the bookstore at midnight so she could buy the next book the very moment it became available. She sometimes imagined herself as the boy who left behind a difficult home life to find an entirely new world. Other times she imagined herself as the girl who was friends with two boys, the girl who always knew all the answers, who was brave, strong, and brilliant. She loved it when she found someone else who shared her interest, and she would go on and on about trivial details in each book and the differences between the books and the movies. Although she was usually exceptionally quiet and serious, talking about wizarding school always brought her out of her shell. Her facial expressions and gestures were animated to the extreme, and she talked nonstop at high volume. Eventually even other devoted fans of the series made an excuse to leave. Olivia's interest, although shared by many, was unusually intense, even though no one recognized this as a characteristic of autism.

Unusual in Focus

Olivia loved robotic vacuum cleaners with an intense devotion. She first became aware of the existence of such things in a television commercial. It excited her so much that she watched the infomercial demonstrations again and again. While shopping with her parents, she made a beeline to the vacuum section and read every word on each box. After researching all of the pros and cons of each model, she knew exactly which one she wanted. She begged her parents to give her one for her birthday, but they thought a twelve-year-old would be happier with a video game. She wasn't. She begged again at Christmas, and finally, when she still hadn't given up on it by her thirteenth birthday, they bought her a robotic vacuum cleaner of her own. She named it Dobby and loved it more than any gift she had ever received. Over the years she collected many models and styles, but her original Dobby was always her favorite. Realizing that other people could never understand how she felt, neither Olivia nor her parents ever talked about it, certainly not to her psychologist, who might think it was crazy. Her intense interest of unusual focus was unknown and unrecognized as a characteristic of autism.

TIFFANY

Unusual in Intensity and Focus

Rocks had fascinated Tiffany for as long as she could remember. When a particular pebble called out to her, she always picked it up, examined it closely, rubbed her thumbs across it, and sniffed it. If no one was looking, she gave it a tiny lick. Every rock had a unique smell and taste, depending on where they had lived before she found them and brought them home to live with her. She had boxes of them, and her collection grew every year. Her mother learned early on that it was useless to try to persuade her to get rid of even the most ordinary ones. To Tiffany, each one was special, and there was nothing ordinary about them. She secretly named them, which was challenging, but she felt they deserved their own names. Sometimes someone who knew about her collection gave her a polished stone for her birthday. Tiffany was always polite, but the store-bought stones did not hold the same appeal for her. They seemed snooty or uppity next to her chosen rocks. As she got used to seeing them, though, she came to appreciate the way the colors shone so clear and strong. While her rough stones felt just right for rubbing her thumb across, she learned that rubbing the polished stones across her lips or eyelids was a pleasing thing to do. Tiffany never left the house without at least one pebble in her pocket.

One time Tiffany was outdoors at a charity event in a line of celebrities being photographed for some worthy cause or other when she spied a rock on the ground. She stared at it, entranced but knowing that she was not allowed to leave the line to go pick it up. That would only draw unwanted attention. Someone was bound to ask her what she was doing, and what could she say? As she worried about how to get that rock without being noticed, she saw a shoe cover it slightly. Someone was standing on her rock! How could she get it now? Looking up to see who had done this thing, she saw Danny wink at her, and then bend down to tie his shoes and discreetly pick up the rock and slip it into his jacket pocket. When he stood, he smiled at her and nodded with another wink. Later he would present it to her as the perfect specimen it was. What a wonderful man Danny was! Tiffany could not imagine a better husband.

HEIDI

Unusual in Intensity

Heidi loved sports. Although the other girls didn't like her much, when she tried hanging out with the boys, she almost fit in. She could rattle off every statistic for every player on her favorite team. From elementary school through high school, boys she knew would ask her random sports trivia questions, and she would recite the answers without a pause. She didn't realize they were using her for their own entertainment. They didn't like her enough to invite her to a ballgame or to hang out after school. The fact that there were other people who seemed to share her interest in sports trivia was enough for Heidi.

Unusual in Focus

When Heidi was four, an uncle gave her his old harmonica, and a new passion was born. She loved the look of it, the feel of it, the smell of the wood, and the taste of the metal. Best of all, though, was the sound she could make. She loved sliding the harmonica up and down across her mouth, playing scales and experimenting with songs. She loved the fact that she could play one note by breathing out, and a different note by breathing in. She was self-taught at first, and then she got every book about harmonicas at the library and bookmarked every harmonica website she could find on the internet. She began collecting them in every color and size, from the smallest Hohner Little Lady to the biggest one she could afford, the 15.5 inch Chromatic.

She realized at some point that most people do not want to hear someone play their harmonica at parties or work breaks, so she quit offering. She did keep a small one on a key chain with her all the time, though, and she pulled it out to play whenever she was stuck at a railroad crossing waiting for the train to pass. What was stressful to most drivers trying to get somewhere in a hurry was a restful oasis of harmony for Heidi.

Behind the Mask

Autistic girls and women often have interests which are similar to those of their peers but much more intense. They also often have unusual interests that would surprise others. The presence of these characteristics of autism may be hidden because they don't want to come on too strong and go on and on about their interest, boring others. They may not like to share their interest in things that others would find weird or even "crazy." Don't assume that because information about these passions is not shared initially that they don't exist, but do persist in asking questions that help girls and women open up about their interests.

➢ When you were a girl, did you have interests that the other girls thought were weird?

➢ Did you try to pretend to be interested in what the other girls liked, even though your own secret interests were much cooler?

➢ Do people ever tell you to stop talking about the things you're passionate about because you don't notice when you go on and on about it?

➢ Do you love to learn about and think about certain things, but you keep them to yourself because people don't understand?

➢ Would some people think you were "weird" or "crazy" if they knew what you are really interested in?

➢ Do you love to go to conventions about your specific interest, where you can find like-minded people who feel the same way that you do?

➢ When you get together with others who are interested in your favorite topics, are you usually the most excited person in the room?

In Her Own Words

"I take an extreme interest in a variety of subjects. Whenever I really become interested in something, I hyperfocus immediately and can research it all day, nonstop. I sometimes temper how much I talk about my interests, depending on my audience, but a lot of the time I don't. I just don't care to talk about my interests to people that don't know anything about them. For instance, I'm not going to talk about antique marbles extensively with my work family, because they know nothing about the subject. Mostly, people are fascinated by my special interests and seem to be impressed with the depth of my knowledge."

— *Nakeba Todd*

Chapter Seven

SENSORY

If It Sounds Like a Duck, Wear Ear Plugs

Hyper- or hyporeactivity to sensory input or unusual interest in sensory aspects of the environment..."

> — *Diagnostic and Statistical Manual for Mental Disorders, Fifth Edition (DSM-5)*

"It was only when my son was diagnosed as autistic that everything finally made sense ... my sequential interests which are unusual in their variety and intensity, my sensory preferences and my absolute need for solitude. Finally understanding that my experience of the world is different ... allows me to understand my needs and ensure they are met ... at this point I love being autistic ..."

> — *Dr. Mary Doherty, autistic doctor*

Most autists have unusual sensory responses, either seeking out or avoiding various sensory experiences. Many have multiple sensory preferences or sensitivities, and they may both seek and avoid a wide range of experiences. Girls and women are often told, "You're just too sensitive," with the speaker assuming sensitivity is a feminine trait taken to the extreme rather than recognizing its role in an autism diagnosis.

Some seek out and are delighted by certain sensory experiences. A visual seeker might find peace staring at a lava lamp. An auditory seeker might put her favorite song on repeat at full volume. A gustatory seeker loves to explore the world of flavor and may have put everything in her mouth as a child. An olfactory seeker finds calm in certain aromas that help her relax and self-regulate. A tactile seeker may surround herself with the softest blankets, stuffed animals, and comfy clothing. A kinesthetic seeker might find joy spinning around and around, and a proprioceptive seeker may feel more grounded and in touch with her body when she jumps on a trampoline.

Others are significantly adversely affected by sensory experiences. A visual avoider may cover her eyes in bright sunlight or become nauseated looking at certain prints or color combinations. An auditory avoider may experience intense pain at sounds that others are only mildly bothered by. A gustatory avoider may have been called an extremely "picky eater" with a very restricted diet. This may be because of the taste of foods, but it may also be the texture, color, or shape. Olfactory avoiders find it almost impossible to tolerate common scents, such as perfumes, cleaning products, and chemical smells. A tactile avoider may be overly bothered by tags in shirts or seams in socks, or by being touched unexpectedly. Kinesthetic avoiders may be clumsy or become dizzy easily in movement activities. Proprioceptive avoiders strongly dislike big hugs and tight clothes.

A person could experience both seeking and avoiding of the same kind of sensory experience in different situations. For example, she could seek auditory input that she can control, such as humming and tapping things, but be excessively startled by unexpected sounds or those which are out of her control, such as a dog barking, the refrigerator making ice, or someone chewing gum. She may love to look at a snow globe for hours but hate going out in strong sunlight. Of course, olfactory and gustatory seeking and avoiding are common; we all prefer some scents and flavors over others, but in our girls and women on the spectrum, the preferences and aversions may be extreme. Let's take a look at how each of our Fictional Female Figures respond to sensory experiences.

Fictional Female Figures

CHEYENNE

Visual and Olfactory Seeking

Cheyenne was a visual seeker. As a toddler she would sit on the floor in the sunshine, watching dust motes floating in a ray of sunshine for hours. In preschool she would sit alone in the sandbox and pick up handfuls of sand, staring as she slowly let the grains of sand drop from her fingers. As she grew older, she discovered snow globes, kaleidoscopes, and lava lamps. They all held a special charm for her, and she could get lost in a reverie while staring at them.

Cheyenne was also a seeker of olfactory input; she loved to stop and smell the roses. Also the lilies, the cookies, the scented markers, and her mother's hair. When she found something that smelled lovely, she stayed with it, dreamily inhaling the aroma with her eyes closed, the rest of the world shut out. When she grew up, she realized that she could help make her life easier if she always had something in her pocket that had a pleasing aroma: a sprig of rosemary or lavender, a few coffee beans, or one of her favorite fabric softener sheets. Any time she needed to block out a bad smell or help herself calm down, she would breathe it in, and the world would smell a little bit sweeter.

Kinesthetic Avoiding

Cheyenne was not an athlete, not by any stretch of the imagination. She walked and ran awkwardly with both arms held straight down at her sides, and she was clumsy at every sport. As soon as she had enough PE units to graduate, she never took another gym class or tried another sport. In fact, she avoided all kinesthetic or movement activities completely.

PENELOPE

Auditory and Olfactory Avoiding

The sound of a hand brushing across a canvas backpack was excruciatingly painful to Penelope. It was difficult for her to believe that no one else heard what she heard or that everyone else was completely oblivious to it.

Also, most perfumes made her feel ill or like she was choking, or they resulted in intense headaches, depending on the chemical compounds used in them.

Penelope banned all canvas and perfumes or colognes from her lecture halls. It was in the syllabus, and woe be to the student who failed to read and abide by her rule. She would walk out of the lecture hall, and if she knew who the culprit was who had broken her rule, their grade would suffer. When someone had the courage to go above her head and ask the department head if she had the power to enforce such a rule, the head sighed. His recommendation was to simply go along rather than trying to challenge her on it. If it made the professor more comfortable in her working environment, why not comply?

AKIKO

Multiple Sensory Avoiding

Akiko was extremely sensory avoidant. She could not abide the sound of a doorbell or the scraping of a fork on someone's teeth while they ate. She had to close her eyes when coming out of a darkened movie theater because the sunlight was so intense, and her parents would lead her carefully to the car. She had an extremely limited diet and would only eat foods that were soft, such as mashed potatoes, overcooked pasta (never al dente), apple sauce, and creamy soup as long as there were no chunks in it. She was also strongly affected by many smells, such as artificial chemical smells, body odor, perfumes, cleaning products, and gasoline. If she accidentally got a whiff of one of these, it triggered a gag reflex and she had to work hard to keep herself from vomiting. Proprioceptive feedback, or deep muscle or joint information, was painful for her, and she couldn't abide tight hugs or turtleneck sweaters. Sometimes she didn't seem aware of where her body was in space, and she often handed an object to someone but then let go of it before they had taken it, so that it fell to the floor. This always surprised her, but she couldn't figure out how to be sure of the timing of passing an object between people. When Akiko was old enough to join the Scout troop at their church, her mother bought a uniform pattern and extremely soft fabric in the Scout color. Even without a diagnosis, her mother knew that Akiko would never tolerate the starched, scratchy uniform. For Akiko, the world was an overwhelming sensory nightmare.

RUTH

Tactile and Kinesthetic Seeking

Petting her cat was Ruth's idea of bliss. It was so soft and sleek, and her hand glided so smoothly across its back. She could pet her cat for hours and feel better afterward, no matter how stressful her day had been. Her cat seemed to understand this and sought her out when she was feeling particularly anxious, settling down on her lap and purring. If her cat was not around, touching anything soft could help her calm down, even stroking her own hair.

Ruth also loved the kinesthetic feedback she got from movement, like rocking or pacing. If she became agitated, reliving some awkward social mishap of the day, she felt like she had to keep her body in motion. If she was in public, she would clench her leg and stomach muscles to keep her from rocking, step outside to walk quickly around the building or block, or go to the restroom and rock in private. She didn't let other people know what she was doing because she thought it made her look crazy, so her counselor never knew that she had these sensory responses.

OLIVIA

Kinesthetic Seeking

Olivia loved the feeling of spinning around. The air rushing past her, the dizziness, the visual effect of the world swirling by again each time she spun. She loved playground merry-go-rounds, swiveling chairs, carousels, and spinning teacup rides. The best part was the way her body felt when she was spinning, as if all was right with her world. Kinesthetic circular motion just felt right to her.

Tactile Avoiding

Art can be messy. Olivia hated the feeling of finger paint, chalk, or glue on her hands. She avoided all of the art activities in school that required her to touch anything "icky." When there was any chance of rain, she bundled up, wearing gloves, scarf, and a hat so no drop of water would touch her hands, neck, or head.

As an adult she owned several pairs of rubber and latex gloves for various household tasks, such as rinsing plates and loading the dishwasher. Tactile avoiding, especially where her hands were concerned, was important to her.

TIFFANY

Multiple Sensory Seeking and Avoiding

Rocks offered Tiffany a variety of sensory experiences. She sought out the olfactory, gustatory, visual, auditory, and tactile aspects of the rocks she loved and collected. She sniffed, tasted, stared at, and touched them repetitively. The feeling and sound they made when she ran her hands through a box of stones, lifted up hands full, and let the stones drop back into the box with their brothers and sisters was unusually satisfying for her.

She also loved watching ceiling fans turning, water running down the sink, and tiny "floaters" in her own eyes. She could spend hours gazing at a lava lamp or twinkling white lights on the Christmas tree. Colored Christmas lights were too harsh and busy for her, but soft white lights that twinkled instead of blinking were perfect.

Other sensory experiences were challenging for her. She tried not to breathe when the makeup artists got her ready for work and was grateful when one of them found a different kind of foundation and base that did not have such a strong odor. If someone dropped a script on the floor, Tiffany jumped and squeaked. One of the production assistants thought it was so cute when she did it that he would intentionally drop a script behind her. That is, until Danny had a quiet talk with him. Danny's minor in psychology helped him to communicate effectively without being threatening or intimidating. He strongly believed that if other people understood that some things really, really bothered Tiffany, they would want to stop doing those things. It seemed to work.

HEIDI

Multiple Sensory Seeking

Heidi was a seeker of all kinds of sensory input. She loved the deep muscle and joint proprioceptive feedback she got from jumping. She craved the feeling of carrying something heavy, whether it was a jug of fabric softener, a backpack, or bags of mail at work. She loved gustatory feedback; as a child she put everything into her mouth, including the cuffs and collars of her shirts. As an adult, she still chewed pens, pencils, and her fingernails. She loved the tactile feedback of water play; she would spend hours as a child holding her hands under running water. It was difficult to get her out of the swimming pool or shower once she got in the water. She loved auditory feedback, from her delighted shrieks as a young child to her passion for the harmonica, which continued into adulthood. Heidi was up for anything, and there was no sensory experience that she didn't want more of. Her lack of sensory aversions made it difficult for her therapist to realize that she had autism. Many people still picture an autistic child as one who covers their ears and eyes and shrinks from sensory experiences, so Heidi was not recognized.

 **Behind the Mask**

It is not at all unusual for autistic girls and women to have intense sensory interests or aversions. Because of their gender, many people brush off girls' sensitivities without recognizing them as characteristic of autism, saying, "She's just sensitive." Autistic girls and women often conceal their sensory-seeking behaviors, and try to be brave when faced with sensory aversions, further masking their autism. Here are some questions to ask to learn more about their relationship with the sensory world.

> **AUDITORY SEEKING:** Do you have a favorite sound, something that makes you happy when you hear it? Do you love repeating certain favorite words or phrases because of the way they sound to you? What sounds or music can calm you and help you feel like yourself again after an especially trying day? When a particular sound or word delights you, and you feel like making the sound or repeating

the word aloud, do you try to keep it to yourself so other people won't think you're weird?

➤ **AUDITORY AVOIDING:** What is the worst sound you could hear? Are there loud sounds that bother you more than other people? Are there specific small sounds that grate on your nerves, like people breathing or chewing? Do you need to cover your ears or wear headphones or earplugs to block the worst noises? When normal noises bother you a lot more than they seem to bother everyone else, do you try to pretend to be fine even though it's painful so that others don't think you're weak?

➤ **VISUAL SEEKING:** As a child, or now, have you enjoyed staring for a long time at visually pleasing images, such as dust particles in sunshine, shadows, your hands, shiny or sparkly things, swirling images like videos of water going down the drain or someone powerwashing a driveway, or starry screen savers, twinkly lights, kaleidoscopes, snow globes, or lava lamps? Could you spend hours staring at your favorite images? Can visual images like these help you regroup and feel better when you've been under stress? Do you try to hide how much time you spend staring at a single image on your computer, hoping people will think you are reading or playing a game rather than getting lost visually? Do you sometimes have trouble recognizing someone's face alone and need to see them from another angle or wait for them to talk before you are sure of who they are?

➤ **VISUAL AVOIDING:** When you look at a drawer full of utensils, or a desk full of papers and other things, or a crowded kitchen cupboard, is it almost impossible for you to find the one thing you are looking for? When lights start flashing, such as strobe lights, do you need to close your eyes? Do you miss visual clues on TV shows unless someone talks about the object that the camera closed in on? If you are trying to listen or concentrate, do you need to close your eyes to block out visual images? Does sunlight hurt your eyes more than it seems to bother other people? Are there certain colors, plaids, stripes, or prints that are so bold that you have to look away or that make you feel nauseated or highly uncomfortable? Do you try to pretend you are fine in these situations because no one else seems to be bothered by the bright light or the patterns that hurt your eyes?

➤ **TACTILE SEEKING:** Do you collect things that are very soft, like blankets, pillows, or stuffed animals? When traveling, do you bring your own pillow and blanket with you? When you are under stress or worried, do you cover yourself with a soft blanket, or hug a pillow or stuffed toy, or pet your cat or dog, because the softness helps you calm down? Are you private about your stuffed animals or blankets because you think others will view this as childish or odd?

➤ **TACTILE AVOIDING:** Are you overly bothered by tags in clothes, seams in socks, or certain fabrics that are too rough? Does it bother you a great deal to touch certain objects like sand paper, or cotton balls, or slick or slimy substances? Do you need to wear plastic, latex, or rubber gloves to do household tasks, or do you find that the gloves themselves feel terrible so you can't wear them? Do you keep these aversions to yourself because you don't want people to think you are persnickety?

➤ **GUSTATORY SEEKING:** Do you love extremely spicy foods and crave lots of flavor? As a child, were you always licking things or people, or putting things in your mouth, or chewing on things like your shirt cuffs or collars, your fingernails, or pencils? Do you still feel more comfortable with something you can put in your mouth, like a pencil, vape pen, or drinking straw? If you still love chewing on things, do you try to do this in private because it looks weird?

➤ **GUSTATORY AVOIDING:** Were you considered a picky eater as a child? Do you still have a limited repertoire of foods you eat? Are your food preferences shaped by how a food looks or feels as well as how it tastes? Do you prefer to go to the same familiar restaurant each time you go out because you know there will be something on the menu you can enjoy?

➤ **OLFACTORY SEEKING:** As a child, did you sniff a lot of things, including things that were not particularly scented? Did you ever sniff people, so that others may have thought you were pretending to be a dog? Do you still find that your favorite scents can help you calm down when things are rough? When you stop to smell the roses, do you try to limit this because other people think it's unusual to spend so much time sniffing a flower?

> **OLFACTORY AVOIDING:** Do you find that some common odors have a strong negative effect on you, more so than others? Do you need to avoid candle stores and the detergent aisle in the grocery store because those scents can be overwhelming for you? Do you try to cover up how sick the smells make you feel because no one else seems to notice the odors?

> **KINESTHETIC SEEKING:** As a child, did you love to swing or spin yourself around for hours? Do you still love the feeling of movement when riding in an open car or boat or riding a Ferris wheel, merry-go-round, or roller coaster?

> **KINESTHETIC AVOIDING:** Do you get motion sickness more than most people? Have you been clumsy and not good at sports? As a child, did you run awkwardly, with your arms straight down, or leaning forward with your arms held out behind you? Would you prefer to sit on the bench and wave at your friends or family when they go on the rides at an amusement park? Do you try to minimize your strong dislike of movement so people won't know how much it affects you?

> **PROPRIOCEPTIVE SEEKING:** Do you crave big bear hugs? Do you feel great when you are jumping or stomping your feet on the floor? When you are stressed, does it help you to lie down flat with as much of your body as possible pressed against the hard floor? Do you prefer your clothing to be tight against your body rather than loose so that you can feel the pressure of long sleeves, long pants, or

a turtleneck shirt? Does it calm you to have someone squeeze you tightly or even lie down on top of you? Are you embarrassed to ask someone to do this for you because it seems weird?

> **PROPRIOCEPTIVE AVOIDING:** Do you hate the feeling of tight clothing constricting you? Have you been told you have a weak handshake, but you'd rather not shake hands at all? Are big hugs too much for you, and you'd rather just wave at your loved ones instead of hugging them? Do you find it difficult to talk to them about this, because you're not sure why you are so averse to hugging someone you love?

In Her Own Words

"Sensory overwhelm is my biggest challenge with autism. Mostly I have found ways to work around them and appear as normal as possible. However, there is one unique sensory issue that can be incredibly difficult for me to navigate. The sound of metal scraping against itself (such as two pieces of silverware sliding against one another) will nearly bring to me my knees. We only have reusable plastic or bamboo utensils in our household to eliminate the possibility of it! At a restaurant, though, it's not so easy. The gentleman at the neighboring table cleans off his knife with his fork after every single bite. I can't block it out. I can't leave and come back after he is done eating. I can't ask him to stop or to eat with a plastic utensil. The response this sound creates in my body is overwhelming. My nerves light on fire, my muscles tense up, my teeth clench, my eyes can't focus, and I can't hear anything other than that noise. In some extreme situations, I have had to make up an excuse to leave. Sometimes, though, I can manage to redirect the awful energy that is going through my body by clenching my fist under the table, slightly swinging my feet, and biting my lip in a hopefully not-too-obvious way. If the sound is temporary enough, this tactic works wonders until it passes.

"I believe neurotypicals may misunderstand this as a preference, like a song that we just don't want to listen to yet again. That couldn't be further from the truth. The touch, sound, or sight of something can cause a nervous system response that will overwhelm the entire system. We are left unable to focus, participate, or cope. We do our very best to make this uncontrollable response as unobtrusive as we can, but it is not always possible. In those moments when it is not possible, we hope and pray for compassion from those around us."

— *Jessica Dawn, diagnosed at age 33*

PART III
ADDITIONAL CONSIDERATIONS

"When I was diagnosed, it just gave me permission to be kinder to my-self...to start to tell people, 'I'm clumsy, but I [don't] mean to be. And being more open about, 'I need you to tell me what I did wrong, and then we can move on from there.'"

— *Hannah Gadsby, autistic comedian*

Chapter Eight

DEVELOPMENTAL
Was ASD Always There?

"Symptoms must be present in the early developmental period (but may not become fully manifest until social demands exceed limited capacities, or may be masked by learned strategies in later life)."

Diagnostic and Statistical Manual for Mental Disorders, Fifth Edition (DSM-5)

"When I was a child, I was not very socially skilled with the other kids, not showing interests with other people, displaying some of the challenging behaviors that a child on the autism spectrum would have."

— *Gloria Mendoza, autistic Technical Quality Manager*

When autistic women seek a diagnosis in adulthood, they are often told that they "can't be autistic" because they weren't recognized as autistic in childhood. Of course, this does not take into account the fact that many of them have been so good at imitating others and masking their unusual characteristics that no one suspected autism. When diagnosticians require parental input to verify autistic symptoms at age four or five, this can be problematic for many autistic women. Some are older and may have only begun to learn about and suspect autism when their children or grandchildren are diagnosed. Their parents may no longer be living. Some parents are in denial and will report that their daughter was perfectly fine throughout their childhood. They are sure that there was never anything "wrong" their little girl. Some parents want to forget or hide the unusual things their daughter may have done, or they fear being blamed for not noticing it sooner. Some still believe that autism is somehow the fault of a cold "refrigerator mother," an old myth which was debunked long ago. Other parents may have autistic characteristics themselves, so they believe "everybody is like that." For whatever reason, parents of adults are often not good reporters about autism. Also, some adults may not want to share their diagnosis with their family until they are ready. Having their doctor contact their parents to ask questions about their childhood would be an unwanted invasion of their privacy.

So how is a diagnostician to meet the requirement under Part C that symptoms of autism must be present in the early developmental period if they can't talk to the parents? Sometimes a woman will have a sibling or childhood friend who is aware of their autistic characteristics during childhood and who they are willing to bring into the assessment process. If no one else is available, ask the woman seeking diagnosis. Adults remember their childhood and can report on their feelings, behaviors, and ways in which they were out of step with the other girls their age. Give them the respect of believing them when they report their own lived experiences.

Remember, too, that the DSM-5 specifically states that the symptoms "may not become fully manifest until social demands exceed limited capacities, or may be masked by learned strategies in later life." It is expected that some autistic people may reach adulthood without being diagnosed, and masking is specifically addressed. It is possible to make a proper diagnosis even if you can't interview her parents. Let's read about our Fictional Female Figures and how they met this assessment challenge.

Fictional Female Figures

CHEYENNE

Cheyenne's autistic characteristics had been present since infancy. Her parents thought she was just bashful, and her unusual behaviors were cute. Her teachers noticed her isolation, but they also saw that she was academically successful and never a behavior problem, so they never referred her for assessment. Her best friend, Bethany, and later her husband, Gabe, both loved Cheyenne for all of her quirkiness and unique ways. The symptoms of autism had always been there, but they were successfully masked and therefore unrecognized and overlooked.

PENELOPE

Because her language and cognition were extremely advanced, no one suspected autism during Penelope's developmental period. With her impressive IQ and precocious interests, she didn't have much in common with other children her age. Her close relationship with her brother was cited as evidence of social functioning; therefore, autism was not suspected, although the red flags were there from the beginning.

AKIKO

Akiko's sensitive nature had been obvious since she was a baby. What her parents didn't realize was that these were also characteristics of autism. Because they knew her sensitivity made her different from her peers in some ways, they assumed that everything different about her was due to her status as a highly sensitive person. The signs were there all along, but autism was never suspected.

RUTH

Ruth had been anxious and depressed since before she started preschool. When she couldn't make friends, her parents and teachers chalked it up to her being so tightly strung or so smart or just not very interested in the other children. Although the characteristics were present during the developmental period, they were not recognized for what they were: symptoms of autism spectrum disorder.

OLIVIA

From her earliest childhood, Olivia had always had difficulty relating to other children her age and felt foreign from them in ways that were difficult for her to express. When she received a diagnosis of obsessive-compulsive disorder (OCD), it explained a lot about the struggles she had lived with her whole life. A lot, but not everything. She still had a nagging suspicion that at her core she was, and had always been, completely different from human children.

TIFFANY

There was never a time when Tiffany did not have autistic characteristics. As a baby, she would rather stare at a ceiling fan than her parents' faces. As a toddler on the set of her TV show, she dutifully echoed every line that was fed to her.   As a child, she neither approached other children nor encouraged them if they tried to talk to her. Even her teen years were unusual. A typical teen pushes back against controls, testing the limits, and prefers peers to parents, but Tiffany felt safest when she was with her mother and her father. She welcomed Danny into the previously closed club only after fifteen years of learning to know and trust him. All of the clues were there if anyone had considered an autism assessment for her, but no one knew what the clues meant. They thought it was just Tiffany being Tiffany.

HEIDI

Heidi's diagnosis of ADHD was certainly not in question. She had always been extremely active and impulsive, and her attention wandered from one thing to another in rapid-fire. Her train of thought was not a lowly loco-motive but a super-speed bullet train. In school, her best friends were in the special education class, and she realized in retrospect that they were prob-ably autistic. It never occurred to her or to anyone that there was anything more than extreme ADHD going on with her, but the symptoms were there, hiding in plain sight.

Behind the Mask

Although they were not identified with ASD until they had reached adulthood, each of our fictional female figures had experienced autis-tic symptoms in childhood that remained unrecognized for years. It is not always possible, when evaluating adults, to get input from parents. Fortunately, lack of parental input does not preclude the possibility of identification. Women can almost always remember things from their girlhood to verify that characteristics associated with ASD were present. They may also remember stories their parents told about "silly" things they did as a young girl. If you are able to talk to their parents, do be aware that many parents may be strongly committed to the idea that there is "nothing wrong" with their daughter. They may minimize or fail to report some behaviors out of embarrassment or a desire to protect their daughter's reputation, lest we think that she is strange or that they are bad parents. In addition, parents were not privy to the inner feelings their daughters hid from the world. Only the individual knows their inner life experience.

Here are some questions to ask the women who come to you for diagnosis, to help you see behind their masks to the autistic symptoms they have hidden for so long.

➤ Think back to your earliest memory involving being around other children your age. What was that like for you?

➤ Did you always feel that you were somehow fundamentally different from the other girls your age?

➤ Was it usually harder for you to make friends, follow social conversations, and get used to new or different things?

➤ Has there been an event in your life, such as a brain injury or global pandemic or other trauma, that clearly happened before any of your autistic characteristics emerged? Did it seem that these autistic symptoms were caused by the trauma?

➤ Does it seem to you that your autistic characteristics pre-dated any trauma that you may have subsequently experienced? Has there been trauma that you believe was related to or caused by your autistic symptoms rather than the other way around?

➤ In your opinion, knowing yourself and your internal responses better than anyone else can know you, do you believe that you exhibited signs of autism during the developmental period, when you were a child?

In Her Own Words

"I believe that my autism was not initially perceived as such. I was a nuisance, a troublemaker; a bothersome little girl with weird interests. My autism was punishable before it was diagnosable. I believed I was an 'alien' or that I was somehow fundamentally broken. That mindset that I carried for so many years still seeps into my adult life."

— Jansen Niccals, disabled artist, diagnosed with autism at age 23

Chapter Nine

IMPAIRMENT
Does ASD Get in the Way?

"Symptoms cause clinically significant impairment in social, occupational, or other important areas of current functioning."

— *Diagnostic and Statistical Manual for Mental Disorders, Fifth Edition (DSM-5)*

"Life is too short to stress the small things anymore."

— *Daryl Hannah, autistic actor*

It doesn't matter how many boxes are checked next to symptoms in the DSM-5; if the symptoms do not cause impairment, then there is no diagnosis. It's as simple as that.

Or is it? If a woman is sitting in our office, smiling, and making eye contact, and they have a job, a husband, and a family, can we assume that their autistic symptoms do not cause impairment? Unfortunately, no. Things are rarely as simple as they appear on the surface. Here is another opportunity to look behind the mask and see how each woman is affected by her autistic symptoms, often internally, in ways that the world cannot see. Social and occupational functioning are usually impaired. Let's look at how each of our Fictional Female Figures is affected by their autism.

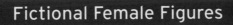

Fictional Female Figures

CHEYENNE

Social Functioning

With both a best friend and a husband, who would imagine Cheyenne was socially impaired? In fact, she felt fortunate to have a lifelong friend like Bethany and an understanding and supportive husband like Gabe. Her life looked perfect. When Bethany and Gabe weren't with her, though, it was a different story. In school and college and while working in the library, she had no idea how to make friends or how to respond to friendly overtures. She was afraid to go to social events or try to meet new people. Any time she wasn't with Bethany or Gabe, she was alone.

Occupational Functioning

Cheyenne managed to survive her one and only job interview at the library, pasting on a smile, nodding, and giving brief, almost whispered responses to their questions. It was so stressful for her that she was sick beforehand and stayed in bed for two days afterward. She was astonished and pleased to be offered a position in spite of how poorly she felt she had presented herself.

She enjoyed the solitary aspects of her job at the library, shelving books, organizing materials, and doing clerical tasks. Any time she was expected to interact with library patrons, though, she got flustered and ended up running and hiding in the bathroom. She worried daily that she would be fired because she couldn't cope with the social expectations of the job she loved.

PENELOPE

Social Functioning

Penelope's social functioning was impaired, in that she did not have any friends outside of her immediate family and she did not have any kind of social or companionable relationships with her colleagues. Had she wanted friends, she would have been clueless as to how to go about initiating a social relationship. She was a failure at interacting with humans other than Peter.

Occupational Functioning

Her occupational functioning was more impaired than Penelope realized. She had been overlooked for department head time after time even though her academic and scholastic achievements, research, and publications far surpassed those of anyone else in any of her three fields of expertise.

The department head needed to be able to work effectively with faculty, staff, students, and the community in order to promote the goals of the university. Penelope didn't care about any of those people or their goals, and everyone knew it. She would have been fired many times over if it weren't for her exceptional worldwide expertise. Although she had achieved full professorship at a young age, that was as far as she progressed up the ladder. She seemed to have hit a solid steel ceiling at the point in her career where social awareness and social skills would have helped her continue to climb.

AKIKO

Social Functioning

Even as an adult, Akiko lived with her parents. She had no friends; the girls she knew in school had moved on, leaving her behind. She didn't know the first thing about how to make friends, even when she did try. It was as if everyone else in the world had gotten a handbook on relationships, but she hadn't gotten hers.

Occupational Functioning

Although Akiko managed to get through the interview process for several entry level positions after graduation, the jobs never lasted long. Sometimes she got fired for too many sick days or for not being a team player, whatever that meant. Sometimes she just couldn't make herself go back, so she quit. The sensory experience of the workplace was too overwhelming, with the sounds of all the other people in the office space talking on their phones, scraping their chairs on the floor, scratching their pens on paper, starting up their computers. The constant hum of the fluorescent lights and the computer wires and HVAC ducts in the walls was painful to her ears. She despaired of ever finding a job she could hold on to in a place that she could stand to spend time in.

RUTH

Social Functioning

Ruth had no friends to speak of. When she did connect with someone, something invariably went wrong. Sometimes she forgot to do "friend" things to keep it going, and the relationship faded away. Other times there was some kind of misunderstanding, her friend was angry about something Ruth didn't understand, and she let the friendship die rather than trying to figure out what could be done to repair it. Everything social was a mystery to Ruth. It exhausted her to think about it, so she didn't.

Occupational Functioning

Ruth's father owned a small company, and she had worked there since graduating from high school. She had a tiny office in the back where she did paperwork, filed orders, sent out invoices, and generally kept the business running smoothly from behind the scenes. She knew how lucky she was. Most of the employees had known her since she was a child. They had no problem with her preference to stay inside her office and avoid social conversations. The fact that she was the boss's daughter may have encouraged their acceptance of her quirks, but the truth is those who had known her the longest had a deep affection for her. However, if anything ever happened to the company and she had to look for a new job, she'd be in trouble. She would have struggled with interviewing, sharing space with colleagues, and participating in team-building activities. For Ruth, staying in the family business was her best and most comfortable option, and she thanked her lucky stars every time she closed the door to her small office and shut out the rest of the world.

OLIVIA

Social Functioning

Olivia's only contacts were her parents and her work. She had no friends at work or in the community. She assumed relationships to be a messy business full of awkward feelings and unpredictability.

Occupational Functioning

Proofreading was Olivia's dream job. When she asked to continue to work from home after her coworkers began returning to the office after COVID-19, she was pleased that her company agreed so readily. She knew that she was much more comfortable and productive in the absence of the social aspects of the workplace. She had no idea that, despite how well she did her job, her supervisors were considering letting her go. She was not a team player and was considered rude and "prickly" in her rare interactions with colleagues. She pointed out even her superiors' errors loudly and tactlessly. Everyone who worked near her in the office was relieved that she would not be returning. The social expectations of how to be a good coworker were unknown to Olivia, and, in fact, she didn't even know that there were so many social rules that she didn't know.

TIFFANY

Social Functioning

Most Hollywood types have active social lives, but Tiffany's was nearly nonexistent. Her parents tried to arrange play dates with her fellow actors during hiatus, but she was never comfortable without a script. By the time she was a teenager, they realized just how vulnerable she was. Since she would never lie or try to hurt someone, she assumed that other people were the same and would have been easy prey for someone to take advantage of. They never allowed her to take a meeting alone or go out to parties unsupervised, which was fine with her. She was grateful to have her parents and Danny looking out for her, and the Vladimir Hinks Society of Good Quirks to understand and accept her as she was. She needed nothing more. However, had she wanted to expand her social circle, she would not have had the skills to make a new friend, or to maintain a friendship over time, or to figure out what went wrong and repair it during rough patches. Understanding relationships was a deficit for her.

Occupational Functioning

While the course of her career was not hampered by disability, the truth is that Tiffany might have had a much more successful career if she had been willing to try for the bigger roles. She was happy playing smaller roles, though, and they supported her financially and allowed her to save for the future.

HEIDI

Social Impairment

Heidi has always been clueless about social skills. She charges in without thinking about what someone else might be thinking or feeling and ends up confused when people are put off by her. Friends she had in school and in the workplace have tended to be neurodivergent themselves, and she doesn't know how to make friends or get along in social settings.

Occupational Impairment

Every time her boss speaks to her, Heidi worries that she may lose her beloved job. She doesn't really understand why, but she keeps getting written up. They tell her it's about "the incident" with one coworker or another without explaining what "the incident" was. They seem to assume that she knows what went wrong. She doesn't. Each new social interaction in the workplace is unique to her, and she doesn't realize which of her words or actions make other people feel uncomfortable. She learned not to ask customers what's inside their package because of a complaint filed against her. She learned not to ask if she can watch a customer open the package she delivered because of another complaint. She learned not to ask a customer how old they are, and then later she learned, in a separate incident, not to ask a coworker how old they are. Later, she learned not to ask a customer their weight. Each social blunder was an island, one more new thing to learn, because she couldn't see the bigger picture, cause and effect, or what each social error had in common with any of the others. She just didn't get it.

 Behind the Mask

Just because someone looks on the outside as if they have their act together socially and occupationally doesn't guarantee that they are not deeply affected by their autistic characteristics. Here are some questions that may help you look behind the mask and learn more about your client's social and occupational functioning.

Social Functioning

➤ Have you ever had the help of a sister, a close friend, or someone else who helped you navigate the social world? For example, someone who introduced you to their friends, encouraged you to go to parties and stayed with you if you were uncomfortable, or played matchmaker to help you find a partner?

➢ If you didn't have someone you were close to who encouraged you to be more socially active, would you still go out to social events or would you be more likely to stay home if you had to go alone?

➢ Have you always felt that you were on the fringe of your friend group, a tolerated hanger-on but not one of the central friends in the group?

➢ Has the world of friendships and relationships seemed like a mystery, the way other people seem to make friends and fall in love so easily, but not you?

➢ Have you lost friends and relationships because of social mistakes or problems that you never really understood?

Occupational Functioning

➢ Most people don't enjoy job interviews, but are they much more difficult for you than they seem to be for everyone else?

➢ Do you have difficulty working for a boss when it appears that you are smarter than they are?

➢ Is it hard for you to keep your criticisms of your supervisors or colleagues to yourself when you see that they are in the wrong or breaking rules?

➢ Do you struggle to understand the social aspect of the workplace and wish that you could just work in peace without being expected to be social, too?

➢ Have you lost jobs because you didn't understand the social complexities at play?

"Thinking back, my peers sometimes treated me like they figured something might be wrong socially, but I think my academic advancement highlighted the more positive attributes of autism and helped me to manage the more difficult ones. I never realized the social deficits I had when I was younger. I never understood why my parents worried about me and said I needed to be more aware and cautious. I understand a bit more now, the social elements that I missed, but I still don't understand it completely and I'm working on it. I do not think seeing the good in everyone is such a bad thing, but I understand how it can make social awareness difficult.

"I have noticed sometimes people treat me differently on jobs. Once, someone at work kind of asked if I was autistic because of my reaction to people being in my space. I thought she was joking. I think she was. She kind of laughed, but she also looked serious in her face. Under extreme pressure, I shut down. With the right support, I flourish. Fortunately, I have amazing mentors."

— *Nakeba Todd*

"I wonder how much easier my life would have been if I had known earlier what was going on with me. I struggle socially and have yet to find an occupation (other than self-employment) that would even begin to accommodate my neurodivergency. I hate to admit that I live with quite a bit of fear in day-to-day life, as I am unable to function by myself, in a society that provides next to no help for autistic adults."

—*Jansen Niccals, disabled artist, diagnosed with autism at age 23*

Chapter Ten

OTHER CONDITIONS

Could It Be Something Else?

"These disturbances are not better explained by intellectual disability..."
— *Diagnostic and Statistical Manual for Mental Disorders, Fifth Edition (DSM-5)*

"There are enough people in the world who are going to write you off. You don't need to do that to yourself."
— *Susan Boyle, autistic singer*

t is important to be aware of other conditions which are similar to autism to determine whether someone's autistic characteristics may be attributed to something different. For example, many children with intellectual disability flap their hands when they are excited, or walk on their toes, or have delayed communication and immature social skills, but this does not mean that they also have autism. (Unless they do.) Are their social skills and language ability commensurate with their mental age, even though they are delayed compared to those of typical same-age peers? If so, it is unlikely that they have autism in addition to intellectual disability. A diagnosis of autism cannot be based solely on the presence of mannerisms such as hand flapping and toe walking, or on communication and interaction skills which are delayed for their chronological age but not for their developmental age.

There are many comorbid conditions that are shared by a large number of autistic people. ADHD, Obsessive Compulsive Disorder (OCD), social and generalized anxiety, depression, and insomnia are just a few. The fact that a girl or woman meets diagnostic criteria for one or more of these disorders does not rule out autism. By following the DSM-5 criteria and questioning her to learn about symptoms which may have been masked, a proper diagnosis may be made or ruled out with confidence.

Fictional Female Figures

CHEYENNE

Cheyenne was always extremely shy, but many other girls are shy without also being autistic. What's different about Cheyenne?

While other shy girls develop friendships in a typical manner once they have become comfortable with someone new, this was not true for Cheyenne. She always felt that she was, at her core, very different from the other girls her age, like an alien who was accidentally left on this planet.

Although she looked on the outside like a quiet, bashful girl indistinguishable from typically developing girls, her internal feelings were very different. She was mystified by the way other girls became friends so naturally while she could never comfortably fit in. She covered up for her lack of social understanding with a fixed smile, mirroring the other girls. She pretended to get their jokes and share their interests from the sidelines, but the other girls at school never invited her to a sleepover or to hang out at the mall with them. It never even occurred to her to take the first step and invite them. It also never occurred to her that the reason she felt so different from neurotypical peers was because she was autistic.

PENELOPE

Clearly Penelope did not have any intellectual or language delay or disability, and there were no other disabilities or conditions that might explain her particular collection of behaviors.

AKIKO

Akiko's extreme sensory responses were called a sensory processing disorder, and she was considered a highly sensitive person. Her other autistic symptoms were less obvious but just as debilitating. Her struggles to make and keep friends, relationships, and jobs, were all connected to her social communication and interaction deficits. As she grew older, she learned to successfully mask the more unusual autistic mannerisms and interests that her parents were embarrassed by, like her fascination with balancing straws. So successfully, in fact, that for years she was unable to be accurately diagnosed with autism spectrum disorder.

RUTH

Like they were for many autists, Ruth's anxiety and depression were recognized and treated early. No one looked behind the mask to see that the root cause of both conditions was her autism. Being autistic in a neurotypical world, aware that everyone else seems to understand subtle, nonverbal cues that you can never quite decipher, can certainly cause anxiety. It is depressing to know that you are different from everyone else you meet and that you have no way of getting by except by pretending to be like them. Masking starts as a survival skill but becomes more and more exhausting over time. Eventually the day comes when the burden of trying to be someone you are not is too much to bear. Fortunately for Ruth, that realization brought her to search online for others like herself, finding answers and support in the autism community.

OLIVIA

It was obvious to everyone right from the start that Olivia had OCD. While her intense interests could be seen as obsessions and her mannerisms might be thought of as compulsions, there was more to her story than the diagnosis of OCD alone could explain. While correct as far as it went, it did not address her disdain for other children or her complete disinterest in any kind of social interaction or relationship. To her, other humans were at best interesting subjects to study and at worst undesirable distractions interfering with a happily solitary life. That was Olivia's autism being masked by the more obvious signs of OCD.

TIFFANY

Working with her tutors on set instead of in a typical classroom environment benefited Tiffany academically. Her sharp memory and ability to repeat facts verbatim meant she was a good test-taker, as long as it was not a timed test, which made her anxious. There were no other conditions which could better explain the unique collection of behaviors and characteristics that made up Tiffany's autism.

HEIDI

No one ever doubted for a moment that Heidi had ADHD. But how could anyone know that she also had autism?

Her social understanding was problematic. Many kids with ADHD impulsively act out and find themselves in the midst of a social blunder before they have time to stop themselves. The difference is they are usually aware of what their mistake was, after the fact. Impulsivity is the issue, not lack of social awareness or understanding. For Heidi, she never knew why she kept getting in trouble. Each social interaction was a mystery to her. She was intensely interested in getting close to people and learning about them, and most psychologists saw this as a reason to reject the possibility of autism. However, for Heidi, her social interest and incessant questioning, trying to learn everything she could about every new person she encountered, was more like an autistic special interest rather than a sign of social strength. Unfortunately, that social interest kept professionals from suspecting autism for many years.

Behind the Mask

Many autistic people have comorbid conditions, some with overlapping symptoms. The presence of these should not get in the way of an autism diagnosis if your client meets the diagnostic criteria. Here are some questions that may get to the heart of hidden autism:

> When you look inside yourself, do you feel that you are in some way different from most other girls or women your age?

> Do you feel that your other diagnoses tell the whole story of you and your challenges in life, or is there more to it? Are there fundamental differences that your other diagnoses don't address?

In Her Own Words

"I had never considered that I may be autistic until I came across an article about a woman who had been diagnosed as an adult. I read her story and was rather blown away at how much we had in common. Her struggles and challenges sounded exactly like mine. I had known something wasn't right for many, many years and sought assistance through my medical doctors and therapist. They all told me that I was just anxious, depressed, wasn't taking care of myself, wasn't resting enough, or that perhaps it was fibromyalgia. I became convinced that I simply had an anxiety problem that I couldn't control."

—*Jessica Dawn, diagnosed at age 33*

Chapter Eleven

THE GENDER SPECTRUM
Embrace the Rainbow

"If someone finds using your pronouns or name difficult, then that is about them and they need to change...You have the right to be who you are...Autism and gender diversity are so beautiful!"

— *Yenn Purkis and Wenn Lawson,*
trans autistic authors

Some studies suggest that a greater number of autistic people identify as LGBTQIA+ compared to the general population. While more studies are needed to learn more about the intersection between the two spectrums, we do know that neurodiversity (ND) and gender and sexual diversity (GSD) are often found together.

It is important to respect what autistic people tell us about their lived experiences and not to discount what they share about their sexual or gender identity based on their autism. If they trust you enough to share personal revelations about themselves, do them the honor of trusting that they know who they are.

Fictional Female Figures

CHEYENNE

Cheyenne is a cisgender, heterosexual woman, also known as cishet. This simply means that she was assigned female at birth and continues to identify as a woman (cisgender) and that she is only attracted to men rather than to other women (heterosexual). In this way she is aligned with the majority of the general population, even though her autism places her in the neurological minority.

PENELOPE

Gender was never something Penelope thought much about. She knew from toddler-hood that she was a girl and Peter was a boy, based on anatomy, and had no further curiosity about it. Romance was something that was culturally prevalent but of no concern to her.

AKIKO

Her whole life, Akiko found the whole idea of sexual intimacy to be unthinkable. She had no desire to get close to anyone, hold hands, or kiss, and romantic movies left her cold. As an adult she learned that there was a name for people who felt as she did: she was asexual, or Ace. She wasn't alone, although she rarely heard anyone discuss it. Apparently people who were heterosexual, homosexual, or any kind of sexual had a hard time understanding that some people just weren't sexual at all. There was nothing wrong with it, it just was, and Akiko was glad to find a name for how she had always felt.

RUTH/RAIN

Ruth had never really felt like a girl. The other girls seemed to be from another planet. For a while she wondered if maybe she was supposed to be a boy, but that didn't feel right, either. She wondered about gender for years, trying to understand it and what people meant by it. Finally, Ruth came to realize that she was nonbinary. No, that *they* were nonbinary. Not she/her, not he/him, just they, themself. They opted out of any gender identification and chose the name Rain rather than Ruth. Even though autism continued to present challenges, at least Rain wasn't also confused about gender anymore. They felt right as Rain, one more drop in the pool of people who did not conform to either gender. It was a good feeling to find others who shared this nonbinary life experience.

OLIVIA

It didn't bother Olivia that she never got asked to prom. She found boys distasteful as a teen, and as an adult the men she met were boorish, intimidating, or just not quite bright. It wasn't until she began spending more and more time with her coworker, Nita, that she finally realized she was a lesbian. No wonder she had never had any interest in guys. Nita, who also had OCD, shared Olivia's commitment to perfection in proofreading. When they moved in together, they maintained separate bedrooms, bathrooms, and offices. Fortunately, they agreed wholeheartedly on how the kitchen should be organized, down to the last teaspoon. Their life was one of peaceful predictability, which they both found to be ideal.

TIFFANY

Although she had never really thought much about romance before Danny declared his love for her, Tiffany knew herself to be a cishet woman: she was correctly assigned female at birth, and she was attracted to men, or more specifically, she was attracted to Danny.

HEIDI/HOWIE

Typical tomboy Heidi had always preferred hanging out with the boys and identified with them but had never heard of the idea of being transgender until after graduation. Reading about it online and conducting some soul-searching led to the realization that Heidi was, and had always been, a male, even though she had been assigned female at birth. She—no, *he*. *He* changed his name from Heidi to Howard, calling himself Howie. He chose his name after the legendary sports journalist Howard Cosell, but secretly also for Howard the Duck, who always made him laugh. Because he had always hated dresses and frilly nonsense, preferring short hair and mannish clothing, there was very little difference in how he looked after he came out as a man. He shut down questions about whether or not he would have surgery or hormone therapy, saying, "Ha! Wouldn't *you* like to know!" It was really nobody's business. The important thing was he felt like himself at long last, no longer like a pretender. His autism still got in the way of his interactions, and he was often confused in social situations. But at least there was one thing he was no longer confused about: he was Howie, the man he had always been, even before he knew it himself.

Behind the Mask

When you have clients who are trans or nonbinary, the most important thing you can do for them is to respect who they are. You should feel honored that they are comfortable enough with you to share personal information about their gender. Once you know, always call them by the correct name and use the pronouns that they shared with you. Learn more about gender if you have not yet received training in working with the LBGTQIA+ community. It's vital to understand your people and the potential risk of harm if you misgender them or use the wrong pronouns when referring to them. They can feel stigmatized, their self-esteem decreases, and the risk for self-harm increases. If you mistakenly use the wrong name or pronoun, simply apologize and move on, resolving to do better in the future. Here are some questions you might ask:

➢ My pronouns are _____. What are your pronouns?

➢ What is your understanding of gender and your own gender identity?

➢ What is your understanding of sexuality and your own sexual orientation?

➢ If you are not cisgender and/or heterosexual, have you come out to the people that you live with or work with?

➢ If you haven't come out yet, are you considering coming out, and if so, do you need support in this process?

➢ Do you feel safe? Are you being bullied or intimidated by others? Is anyone hurting or abusing you, or are you afraid that they will if you share your identification with them?

➢ Are you in danger of losing your home or your job if the people you live with or work with learn about your orientation or identity?

➢ What help do you need to be safe?

In Their Own Words

"I am an autistic transgender man. I was assigned female at birth and was raised as a young woman well into my teenage years. My journey with my gender identity was taken more seriously than my journey to find an autism diagnosis as an adult. I do believe that autistic trans and gender non-conforming people have a more intimate relationship with themselves and therefore may come to the conclusions about their identity with more insight and accuracy than allistic trans people. I believe that now, my queerness and autism wind around each other like clock hands. They are part of the same machine but function in different capacities and should be respected as two separate journeys."

— *Jansen Niccals, disabled artist diagnosed with autism at age 23*

"I was 23 years old when I first began to wonder if I might be autistic. Being bisexual was one of my characteristics, among many, that led me to believe I might be autistic. I was aware that many people who are on the spectrum are also a part of the LGBTQ+ community. It wasn't until I really began to understand my social struggles as being primarily an autistic trait that it started to all make sense. I didn't feel good or bad about being autistic, it just feels like a fact of life. I am excited to connect with the autistic community."

— *Reese Dawson*

PART IV
DIAGNOSIS

"Core diagnostic features are evident in the developmental period, but intervention, compensation, and current supports may mask difficulties in at least some contexts. Manifestations of the disorder…vary greatly depending on the severity of the autistic condition, developmental level, and chronological age; hence, the term spectrum."

> — *Diagnostic and Statistical Manual for Mental Disorders, Fifth Edition (DSM-5)*

"I had a life-changing moment when I discovered, at the age of fifty, that I'm on the autism spectrum…This was the greatest gift I ever received, learning why I am the way I am."

> — *Anita Lesko, autistic author*

Chapter Twelve

FINDING ANSWERS

Opening Doors

"Today I have a full and meaningful life. I am content and happy and I am still just as autistic as I have always been."

— *Judy Endow, autistic author*

Finally being diagnosed can be an incredible gift, to know at last that there is a name for the difference you have recognized. It is not necessarily an unmixed blessing. Many emotions may come and go, taking their turn at the forefront.

Worry. Will people treat you differently if they know you are autistic? There is no need to disclose your diagnosis to anyone that you don't trust with this knowledge.

Fear. Will your life get worse in a downward spiral that you won't be able to turn around because of your autism? There is no evidence that this will happen. Many autistic people have happy and fulfilled lives. They face the inevitable challenges we all do with a commitment to making changes as the need arises, to stay on track to success. Seek out help when you need it.

Regret. Would your life be different today if you had known about your autism years or decades ago? There is no way to know how the past might have been different, but I hope you can look forward to a future with greater self-knowledge, understanding and support.

Anger. Why didn't your parents get you tested in early childhood? Why didn't your therapists or doctors recognize what is now so clear? Since we can't go back in time and change anything in the past, it will be good to learn to give up the negative emotions when you can, allowing more focus and energy to be directed toward the positive aspects of your diagnosis.

Relief. There is nothing "wrong" with you. You are not failing at being "normal"; you are surviving and thriving while autistic. And you're not alone. Many, many autistic women are realizing that they've masked who they are for their entire lives, and now they're exhausted. It's wonderful to finally feel free to drop the camouflage and be yourself, quirks and all.

Excitement. You have a brand new identity, and it can feel like a whole new world has opened up to you. You may find other autistic women who share similar experiences with you. Perhaps they have words of wisdom and advice, having walked this path before.

Self-esteem. You are not weak for being overwhelmed by sensory and social experiences. This is autism, it's hard, but you are strong. You deserve the right to manage or limit your exposure to situations you can predict will be overstimulating.

Hope. Knowing your diagnosis may open doors to understanding, acceptance, and needed accommodations.

Mission. If you have been helped, are there ways in which you, in turn, may help others? Reaching out to women struggling with their diagnosis, letting them know that they are not alone, is an important gift you are now in a position to offer. You have been on a journey of wondering about your differences, seeking help, and finding your answers in this diagnosis. Others will follow.

 Fictional Female Figures

CHEYENNE

When she was in college, Cheyenne learned about autism in one of her childhood developmental classes. It sounded so familiar to her, she wanted to find out if she herself might be on the spectrum. Although hesitant, she finally gathered her courage and told her family doctor that she thought she was autistic. He laughed and told her she couldn't possibly be autistic, because she made eye contact with him. Cheyenne felt humiliated and frustrated. She had worked so hard to force herself to look at him, or at least the spot between his eyebrows, because she knew that was what people expected from her. She always wanted to do the right thing and hated the thought of disappointing anyone. Unfortunately, her ability to fake eye contact was successful, while her ability to self-advocate was practically nonexistent. After the pronouncement that she couldn't be autistic, while her doctor was still chuckling and shaking his head, Cheyenne apologized and left.

Years later, she still could not shake the feeling that there was something fundamentally different about the way she thought and responded to the world. The more she read about others with similar experiences, the more autism kept coming up in all of her searches. She finally shared her suspicions with Gabe, who was completely supportive. Being a bit out of step himself, he had occasionally wondered if he might have Asperger's but decided he probably just had ADHD. Cheyenne, on the other hand, shared a lot more similarities with autism than he did. Together, they researched diagnosticians who specialized in assessing adults for autism rather than those who mostly worked with children. Among those, they looked for the ones who mentioned diagnosing women. There weren't many, but they found someone that Cheyenne thought she would be comfortable working with. Bethany was also on board, and she volunteered to be interviewed to share about Cheyenne's autistic symptoms during childhood, since they'd been best friends for as long as they could remember.

At the end of the process, Cheyenne received a diagnosis of autism spectrum disorder. This explained so much of her struggle throughout her lifetime. It was a huge relief for her to finally know that there was nothing "wrong" with her. She wasn't a failure at being "normal"; she was doing great while autistic.

PENELOPE

The time came when there had been too many complaints from students, teaching assistants, and colleagues. Penelope's behavior was offensive, her apparently arbitrary rules were seen as a threat to the students' freedom, and everyone wanted her gone.

She was tenured, which made it extremely difficult to fire her. If there were cause, though, a case could be made to ask her to leave the university, which was what was demanded.

Penelope would walk out of the lecture hall any time she smelled even a whiff of perfume, including scented shampoo or deodorant if the person were in the front row. If someone had a canvas backpack or jacket and brushed a crumb off of it with their hand, she slammed her book shut and walked out. This pattern could be seen as abandoning her classes, which was potentially cause for termination.

The deans got together to discuss the problem, but she was such a widely recognized genius in all three of her fields of expertise, it would be a huge loss to the university should they remove her. One dean brought up the possibility that she might be autistic, and if this were true, there were legal protections and accommodations that they could make to ensure her continued tenure with the university. It was decided that the department head would broach the subject with her and respectfully request that she consider autism assessment.

Penelope listened silently to all that he told her, and he did not sugarcoat the complaints that had been filed against her. After he made the recommendation that she be tested for autism, she nodded once and walked out without a word. He worried that she was offended, but that was not the case. She knew there was nothing wrong with being autistic. Peter was a perfect human being, and he was autistic, so she would be proud to share his brain difference as well as his DNA.

Penelopé went straight from the department head's office to call Peter's case manager and ask for a referral for a diagnostician skilled in evaluating highly intelligent autistic women. The assessment process revealed that she was, indeed, autistic in spite of her many strengths. Because her social and sensory responses were due to an acknowledged disability, she was able to seek and receive workplace accommodations through the Americans with Disabilities Act (ADA). Her tenure at the university was safe.

AKIKO

Akiko felt like a failure. She still lived with her parents, and she couldn't hold down a job. She was so sensitive that everything bothered her, and she felt pushed to the limit or into a meltdown on an almost daily basis. She began searching online for other people like her, hoping to find someone who could understand and relate to her, who wouldn't think she was weird or crazy. Searching for other "highly sensitive people" led her to others who shared her intense sensory reactions. Many of the women she met online were autistic, and some seemed to think that she might be, too. When she said she had never been tested for autism, they told her to go online and sent her links to free autism quizzes. Every quiz she took told her that she was highly likely to be autistic, and every article she read confirmed that possibility. She was invited to join a Facebook group of autistic women and met more and more people like her. They welcomed her into their community and assured her that she didn't need a formal diagnosis to belong. Self-diagnosis was respected. Among these autistic women, Akiko felt that she was part of a group, at long last.

When Akiko talked to her parents about autism, they told her that they had suspected autism briefly when she was a toddler, but her pediatrician hadn't seen a need to follow up. When she started school, they had said she was doing fine academically so she didn't need to be tested for anything. Now her parents felt guilty that they hadn't pushed harder. Akiko forgave them and said she got to be so good at camouflaging her autistic symptoms that it was no wonder no one saw them. Her parents offered to pay for her to get a proper diagnosis now, since they felt they had failed to do the right thing before. At first she resisted, until she learned that having a diagnosis could open the door to workplace accommodations and allow her to get a job. She was tired of being dependent and wanted to work, if she could control the sensory problems that made her previous jobs impossible. It was a happy day in their household when Akiko finally got a diagnosis of autism spectrum disorder, with recommendations for workplace accommodations that would allow her to become more independent.

RAIN

No one doubted that Rain was both anxious and depressed. It was hard living in a world that felt so foreign, and it was depressing to think that maybe nothing would ever change. Then their psychiatrist retired and Rain was assigned to someone new. The new psych had to ask them a lot of intake questions, since she was starting from zero to get to know Rain. She had a lot of questions about Rain's childhood and social life. When asked if they had taught themself to make or "fake" eye contact, or if they had practiced making facial expressions in front of the mirror, or if they had pre-planned scripts of what to say in any social situation, Rain said, "Of course. Doesn't everyone?" As it turned out, "everyone" didn't approach life the way Rain did, but many autistic people did. It took Rain a long time to accept the new psychiatrist's suggestion that they were on the autism spectrum. Still, the more Rain discussed it in their sessions, the more they read and learned about autism, the more it became clear. Rain was autistic, and always had been. It was a freeing revelation, and it opened doors to a better understanding of themself and the way they interacted with the world.

OLIVIA

Transitioning to working from home during the COVID-19 pandemic was wonderful for Olivia. So much so that she wondered why she responded so differently than did Nita and their coworkers who bemoaned the need for sheltering at home. She had been working with a counselor on issues related to OCD, and the strategies she learned were helpful, but she felt there was more to learn. OCD didn't feel like the answer to everything that she struggled with. The longer she worked with her counselor, the more comfortable she became, until finally she started sharing her more unusual autistic-like characteristics. In time, her counselor agreed that OCD described who she was in part, but that autism was probably also appropriate. She referred Olivia to a specialist in identifying autism in adults, and the diagnosis was confirmed. Although it took her a while to get used to it after so many years of identifying with OCD, Olivia eventually embraced autism as an important aspect of her true self.

TIFFANY

Danny's MBA came in handy when Tiffany and her parents asked him to take over as her business manager. They didn't trust anyone else, and he took the responsibility seriously. His undergraduate minor in psychology had been helpful in his ability to work with difficult show business people and in negotiating solutions that worked out for all parties involved. The longer he worked closely with Tiffany, though, the more his mind kept going back to his Abnormal Psych class, where they had introduced what had been called Asperger's syndrome at that time. So many similarities between Tiffany and the case studies were hard to ignore.

One day he called up his old professor and met him for coffee to talk about his concerns. The more he laid out the behaviors and social and sensory responses of his hypothetical unnamed "friend," the more he and his professor became convinced that autism spectrum disorder was a strong possibility.

Danny didn't know how to bring it up to Tiffany and her parents, so he decided that on one of their family movie nights he would bring the DVD of the movie about Temple Grandin's life as a successful autistic adult.

"Just like me!" Tiffany exclaimed at many of Temple's responses. Danny just nodded. She asked if she was autistic too and wanted to find out. Her parents were not so easy to convince, but Danny let them know that he didn't think there was anything "wrong" with Tiffany; an assessment would just give them more ways to better meet her needs and make life smoother for her. They found a psychologist who specialized in diagnosing adult women with autism spectrum disorder, and in a few months, Tiffany had her answer: she was autistic.

HOWIE

At work, the guy Howie most enjoyed having lunch with was Bob. Bob usually worked at the desk, weighing packages and selling stamps. He had a very rigid script he used for every customer, which included apologizing for the wait even when there was no line at all. Bob was tall and thin, and he moved and spoke slowly. When he wasn't on script, he rambled, going on about his different interests or what he had read that morning. Howie, on the other hand, described himself as a "fire hydrant," a short, solid cylinder, and he moved and spoke at top speed. Despite these outward differences, the two became great friends. They easily related to the twists and turns of the other's conversational style and got very animated when discussing their favorite television shows. After several months of sharing lunch breaks, Bob mentioned that he had Asperger's, which he said was a kind of autism that didn't exist anymore, but he still felt like an Aspie. Howie hadn't heard of this. He laughed hysterically and shouted, "Ass burgers?!?" three times at top volume. Then he apologized profusely six times until Bob told him he could stop.

Howie went home that night and started researching online. He was amazed at how closely he related to so many of the characteristics. When he told Bob the next day that he thought he might be autistic, Bob said, "Of course." Howie really wanted to know if he was actually autistic, so Bob referred him to his own psychologist. She formally diagnosed Howie after two sessions and a lot of paperwork and questionnaires. Howie was surprised, because he had always thought he just had ADHD, but the psychologist explained that lots of people have both ASD and ADHD. The news threw him for a loop at first, but talking it over with Bob helped him to accept the new diagnosis. It really did explain a lot.

Behind the Mask

Many girls and women may come to you for diagnosis, hoping for answers to the struggles they have lived with their whole lives. Here are some questions that may be helpful to ask as you seek answers together:

➤ Do you feel that you wear a mask in public so that people can't see the real you?

➤ Why do you believe you wear this mask? Is it because you don't want people to know how different you are or to think you're weird or alien?

➤ As you grow older, is it becoming more difficult to maintain the mask, so that you are exhausted at the end of the work day and have no energy left for your family or your own interests?

➤ How did you come to seek autism assessment? Did you read about it or find groups online that you could relate to? What was it about those groups, or the things you read about autism, that you recognized in yourself?

Do not allow the presence of other comorbid conditions to keep you from conducting a comprehensive ASD assessment. Don't be fooled by the survival strategy of masking their autistic characteristics which women have developed, whether intentionally or not, as a way to get by and try to fit in. The women who come to you for help are counting on you to help them learn the truth about themselves. Thank you for the important role you play in their quest for self-understanding.

In Their Own Words

"Being diagnosed with autism has made a big difference. I get sensory over-load with loud noises such as emergency vehicles, concerts, and people talking too loudly. I used to try to act like it didn't bother me, but as soon as I was alone I would completely shut down and be exhausted for the rest of the day. It was unsustainable.

"Now that we know about my diagnosis, I have a great support team. When loud noises occur, they are willing to leave the area with me, or to help me stay and get through it. For example, when we're talking and a fire truck goes by, they stop the conversation and give me a couple minutes to recuperate, and then ask if I'm ready to continue. This means a lot."

— Molly

Chapter Thirteen

NOW YOU KNOW...
What Now?

"My diagnosis was a relief. I no longer have to think of myself as being weird. I'm not weird. I'm only acting in a way that's consistent with how my brain works. It would actually be weird for me to act any other way!"

— *Kara, autistic woman, diagnosed at age 44*

Once a woman receives a diagnosis of autism spectrum disorder, that's not the end of the story. Rather, it's the beginning of understanding herself, of accepting and appreciating herself, and of learning new ways to function and succeed as an autist in a neurotypical world. This chapter is written with the newly diagnosed cis woman, trans woman, or non-binary person in mind. If you are a professional reading this, consider sharing these considerations with your client after the diagnosis. Now that she knows, what now? What are the next steps along her personal journey of autism awareness, acceptance, and advocacy?

Sharing the news with others is an important step along the way once you have been diagnosed. With whom should you disclose this news? Who do you trust? Who needs to know? What are the potential risks and benefits for disclosing or keeping your diagnosis private? It's important to think this through before sharing it with the world, because once you tell someone something, you can't un-tell them. So consider whom you want to include into your inner circle. A risk-benefit analysis is an important step in making the decision, to disclose or not to disclose.

RISKS

We can't know in advance all of the potential risks of disclosure, but we can hypothesize. What is the worst-case scenario if you choose to disclose your diagnosis to someone? Could you lose a friendship? Might a family relationship be strained? Is it possible you could lose your job or a scholarship? Will people look at you differently if they know you have this diagnosis? We know there is nothing wrong with being autistic, but before you disclose your diagnosis to someone else, try to predict how they might react. Limited understanding of autism and belief in myths or stereotypes can be improved with knowledge. Consider sharing books, movies, or television shows with autistic characters with people you are considering disclosing your diagnosis to. What is their take on the autistic character? Do they know the difference between a stereotyped computer geek and an actual autistic person? It can feel safer to wait until you know more about how someone might react to autism before you open up about your own diagnosis.

BENEFITS

Just as the potential risks of disclosing your autism are unknown, so too are the possible benefits. In the best-case scenario, you may find acceptance and understanding in your family and close friendships. You may find that your partner becomes more solicitous, asking if a situation is too sensory-aversive or if you need to leave a party early. It's possible that your coworkers will be more respectful of your need for quiet and solitude to do your best work. I hope that all of these things and more will be true for you, but you are the only one who can decide when and with whom to disclose your autism diagnosis. So how do you decide?

CUPS

A strategy for disclosure found in *Independent Living with Autism: Your Roadmap to Success* (Marsh, 2020) suggests that the acronym CUPS may be used when deciding whom to tell. CUPS stands for Closeness, Understanding, Professionalism, and Support.

CLOSENESS: Is the person you're considering sharing your diagnosis with close to you? A roommate, family member, partner, or best friend? If you have known them for a long time and you trust them, consider sharing your diagnosis with them. If this is someone you just met but hope to be close to, or someone you've know a long time but with whom you don't feel emotionally safe, you are not obligated to share anything with them. You may feel close to a parent, but if you know that they will disagree with the diagnosis, consider keeping your own counsel. You don't owe them this private information unless you choose to share it. If your history with them tells you they will give you negative or critical feedback and you will end up feeling worse, keep it to yourself. On the other hand, if you have a roommate or partner you live with, someone that you have a long-term relationship with, consider sharing. It could be helpful to your ongoing comfort to be able to un-mask around them, to be yourself and have them accept you as you really are.

UNDERSTANDING: Does this person understand what autism is? Do they realize that autism in women looks different than it does in men? If not, are they interested in learning more about you and what helps you cope with social or sensory stressors? If they don't seem amenable to understanding, maybe you don't want to share. On the other hand, knowledge is key to opening the mind to new ideas, and if they are open to increasing their understanding of you, you might find that telling them about your diagnosis improves your relationship.

PROFESSIONAL: If you have a job or are a full-time student, seriously consider whether and how much to share professionally. If you need accommodations for work or school, then the human resources office at your work or the disabled students office at your school will need to be told about your diagnosis. This may or may not mean telling everyone in your professional circle so that your coworkers or classmates may be led to cut you some slack if you're having a bad day. It may mean telling only HR, your direct supervisor, and your professors. Consider how your coworkers or classmates may react. Will they treat you differently if they know you are autistic? Maybe. Or maybe not. If you have a trusted mentor or counselor, consider discussing this issue with them.

SERVICES: If you will need any specialized services as a person with a disability, then you must disclose your diagnosis to the appropriate service providers. Will you need legal assistance, job assistance, housing, or other supports? A diagnosis opens doors to necessary services.

If and when you tell your family and those closest to you, be prepared for a wide range of responses. Remember, if you started this autism assessment process on your own and they haven't been involved so far, it may be brand new information that's difficult for them to process. It took you time from the first article or book on autism you found until you finally sought and received a diagnosis. It will take your loved ones time to digest and think about this information before they are 100% on board. Hopefully, over time, they will accept your diagnosis and actively seek to help accommodate for social or sensory challenges that you may face. Read on to see how the families of our seven fictional figures responded.

 Fictional Female Figures

CHEYENNE

Gabe was right beside Cheyenne when she heard the news of her diagnosis, so she didn't have to worry about telling him or what his response would be. They both felt relieved and a bit excited to have this new information. Cheyenne didn't hesitate to tell Bethany, and as Cheyenne had expected,

Bethany was super supportive. She had already started buying books about autism even before it was official so she could learn more about her best friend/sister-in-law.

Telling Cheyenne's parents was another thing. She wasn't sure how they would react, but she knew she couldn't keep this from them. They had been in her corner for her entire lifetime, smoothing the way for her and advocating for accommodations without knowing that there was a name for what Cheyenne experienced and that it was more than simple shyness.

Cheyenne and Gabe decided to invite her parents and Bethany and her husband over for dinner and share the news with them then. At first, her dad said, "No way!" There was nothing wrong with his daughter. Gabe jumped in to agree wholeheartedly: there was nothing whatsoever wrong with Cheyenne. And she was autistic. Nothing wrong with that. Her mother got a little teary-eyed and asked if this was her fault. Cheyenne was happy to tell her that autism is not caused by parenting, it's just the way her brain is, and it's certainly nobody's fault. Although she still had a lot of trouble interacting with people, she felt that she could learn skills and relaxation strategies to reduce her anxiety when she wanted to get out and meet people. On the other hand, sometimes she would prefer to avoid social activities that involved new people, and that was fine, too. She felt as if she finally had permission to be comfortable with herself.

In the weeks that followed, as Cheyenne's parents read and learned more about autism and talked to Cheyenne and Gabe about it, they came to embrace this diagnosis. It was one more expression of who their daughter was, and that was worth celebrating.

PENELOPE

Once she had her diagnosis, Penelope's department head was able to make the case to the university deans that her tenure could not be terminated based on factors related to her disability.

For her part, she began working with a psychologist to learn to improve her social skills in the areas that were most important to her. The psychologist didn't try to tell her what she should work on but respected her enough to follow her lead and provide information on how to run her own self-management program. She only worked on the behaviors that she decided she wanted to change, such as greeting colleagues and students appropriately and giving feedback when she had understood what someone had told her. It made sense to her that these behaviors could have a positive effect on her career.

Having something else in common with Peter made Penelope happy in some new way. She threw herself into learning about how autism affected her differently than the way it affected her brother, just as she devoted herself to learning any new thing, enthusiastically and wholeheartedly. Perhaps her fourth PhD would be in disability studies.

AKIKO

Although they had been completely on board for the autism assessment, Akiko's parents were unexpectedly dubious after the diagnosis. They had hoped that the testing would show that Akiko only had a sensory processing disorder and was a highly sensitive person. It came as a surprise when the psychologist did not rule out autism, as they had expected. Instead, he stated that autism was her primary disability, with sensory processing simply one of the symptoms of autism rather than a stand-alone diagnosis. As surprised as they were, they loved Akiko and wanted to be supportive, so they didn't disagree with the diagnosis.

For Akiko, it was a huge relief to finally relax and be herself at home. All her life she had tried to hide her struggles, tried to be calm when faced with sensory overload, to be quiet and watchful when in any social situation. She had kept quiet for so long, she was more than ready to embrace this diagnosis. She made friends with other autistic women online and learned from them different stims and strategies that had proven helpful for others.

Her parents were taken aback when she started stimming in new ways, flapping her hands, flicking her fingers, and spinning around on an office chair for long periods of time. These movements brought her peace, but not her parents. Finally they accused her of putting on autistic behaviors since getting the diagnosis, "faking" it because she wanted to be seen as more autistic than she really was, in their opinion. This was so hurtful to Akiko, she went to her room and stayed there for several days, only coming out to get food.

Eventually she prepared a response to her parents. She told them that she had always been this autistic, but that her whole life she had been "faking" being "normal." If they saw more autistic-like behaviors now, it was because she finally trusted them and felt comfortable enough to be herself. If she got ideas from other autistic women online, it was in search of solutions to feeling out of sync with the world, and a lot of the new stims really helped her to feel grounded and self-regulate. With her new diagnosis, she planned to seek disability services and supports for job training and employment, and eventually for help getting housing so she could move out of her parents' home and live independently at last. Before her diagnosis, she had felt depressed and worthless and couldn't see a future where she could be independent, but now, everything had changed. A new world had opened up for her, and she wished her parents would be supportive rather than critical.

It was hard for her to say all that, but she had written it down and practiced until she could do it. Her parents could see how deeply she felt about this, and they began to remember some of the early behaviors that they had ignored and kept silent about because they didn't fit their idea of a perfect daughter. At last, they began to accept their daughter as perfect just the way she was, stims and all.

RAIN

Rain didn't have one big "Aha!" moment of diagnosis. They discussed autism with their therapist for months, and eventually it just seemed obvious that they were autistic. They didn't feel the need for a formal assessment and clinical diagnosis; self-diagnosis was good enough. Who else could know them as well as they knew themself? Since there was no single moment of knowing, there was no big "coming out" event where Rain told their parents or coworkers. It seemed unnecessary. Everyone they lived and worked with accepted them as they were without needing a diagnosis or asking for accommodations. It just never occurred to Rain to tell anyone about what went on in their psychologist's office. Disclosing a diagnosis was not needed for them to have their needs met, so they never disclosed it. Keeping it private was the right choice for Rain.

OLIVIA

When Olivia shared her diagnosis with her parents and her partner, Nita, she was surprised by their responses. Her parents brushed it off, saying, "OCD, ASD, it doesn't matter. You are who you are." They hinted that they thought she was "diagnosis shopping" and just trying to get attention. Since attention was the last thing Olivia ever wanted, this confused her, but her parents shut the door on any further discussion.

Nita actually seemed offended that Olivia wanted an additional diagnosis beyond the OCD that they shared. They had this in common. Why would Olivia try to dig up something to make them different?

Olivia was hurt by their responses, and for a long time she didn't bring it up. Eventually she found that pretending to be who everyone expected her to be was exhausting. Masking to help them feel more comfortable came at the expense of being who she was.

Finally she sat them all down around a table and gave them each a copy of her psychologist's report diagnosing autism. The report spelled everything out more clearly than Olivia could explain it. She watched anxiously while they each read it. After that, they were more open to discussing autism and what it meant to Olivia. Instead of getting frustrated with her when she struggled with crowded social situations or sensory overload, they asked if she was okay or if she needed anything. If she needed to be alone, they didn't get their feelings hurt or take it personally. What a relief to stop hiding behind a mask at long last and to just be herself.

TIFFANY

Knowing she was autistic was something that took some getting used to. Tiffany started reading books written by autistic women and secretly following groups online to read about others' reactions to their own diagnoses. Sometimes she cried remembering conversations from her own past. Once another teen actor had said something to her that she had interpreted as friendly but realized as an adult that it had been mean and intended to put her down. The others had probably been laughing at her, not with her. Sometimes she cried out of relief that there was nothing wrong with her except autism, and Danny kept telling her there was nothing wrong with her, period. Sometimes she cried reading other autistic women's stories, especially if they didn't have the support system that Tiffany was grateful for. Danny was always there to put his arms around her and just hold her, not too tightly, not too loosely. His hugs were just right and always made her feel centered and safe.

At the next meeting of the Vladimir Hinks Society of Good Quirks, Tiffany told her friends that she was autistic. Her pronouncement was met with, "Of course," "Me, too," "Congratulations!" and "Welcome to the club. We're all quirky here." She laughed as she realized that she had inadvertently been drawn to people who were so much like her that they all shared the same neurodivergent diagnosis. What a relief to just hang out and be herself without self-censoring.

Tiffany kept seeing the psychologist who had diagnosed her, and she was learning strategies to help her cope with sensory experiences and deal with social events. The psychologist let her take the lead on what she wanted to work on and never tried to get her to change anything about who she was. If she wanted to rock and shake her hands, she should keep on doing it. Maybe one day soon she would feel comfortable enough to stop hiding in the bathroom when she needed to stim. She learned self-advocacy and how to set boundaries. Every new thing she learned about her autism and herself left her feeling more and more at home with who she was. She was like a perfect polished stone, unique and deserving of her place on the planet, just like every pebble in her collection.

HOWIE

Of course Howie's best friend, Bob, readily accepted Howie's autism diagnosis with no surprise. When Howie tried to tell his parents, though, it was more difficult than he thought it would be. They were still not used to him being a man, calling him Heidi, and suggesting that this was a phase rather than who he really was. They treated autism the same way, as if this was his new hobby and that he would soon get over it.

Howie knew he would never "get over" being an autistic man. He knew who he was. He decided to give his parents more time to get used to all these new ideas. He shared a few books and articles about autism and transgender information, but he never pushed to find out if they read them or not. He hoped that in time they would get used to and accept him as their autistic son, no longer their hyperactive little girl. He was still the same person he had always been, but now he knew more about himself. He liked the guy he had grown up to be.

Beyond the Mask

DIAGNOSTICIANS

If you are a mental health professional, a therapist, psychologist, or counselor who works with women, I hope this book helps you to open your eyes to the many divergent ways that autism presents in female patients. When a woman comes to you questioning whether she might be on the autism spectrum, respect her enough to take her seriously, even if you can't yet see the symptoms of autism for yourself. Be assured that there is much below the surface of an autistic woman who has masked successfully her whole life. Be appreciative of the courage it took her to bring this up.

Ask the probing questions that will allow you to see the woman behind the mask, the autism which has been so well hidden.

Ask the deeper questions. Rather than simply noting her eye contact as you observe it, ask her if she taught herself how to make or fake it. How does eye contact feel to her? How difficult or exhausting is it?

If she has a job or family or seems capable of carrying on a conversation with no observable difficulty, ask her how difficult these things are for her. Ask her specifically if she has masked or camouflaged her true self in order to fit in. Ask her if she feels, at her core, different from other girls and women, and what that difference is like for her.

Be patient. Don't rush to rule out autism by finding one or two things that she seems to be good at. Look into every point in the DSM-5 criteria and discuss each one with her.

FRIENDS AND FAMILY

If you are a friend, partner, or family member of a girl or woman who may have autism, you play a vital role for them. It is in your power to help them live a more comfortable and peaceful life.

Believe them when they tell you how they experience the world, even if you experience it very differently. If your friend, wife, sister, or daughter says that going to the grocery store is a sensory nightmare, don't tell them, "It's not so bad. You're just too sensitive." Just because it's not so bad for you does not mean it is tolerable for them. Yes, they are extremely sensitive, but this is not a choice they make. The way their brain and nervous system respond to typical sensory experiences is actually different from the way you and I experience the same things.

Believing them is a precious gift that is in your power to give your loved one. If they say they can't handle a grocery store, rather than shaming them or urging them to push past their feelings and just do it, help them find alternatives. Many stores offer curbside or parking lot pickup, so it is possible to stay out of the store altogether. Some grocery staples can be delivered in the mail or by a delivery service. There may be people in your circle who would trade tasks with her. Someone might make phone calls for her in exchange for baked goods or go to the store for her in exchange for her babysitting their children at home during the shopping trip.

The important thing is to believe her when she opens up to you, thank her for trusting you enough to share herself and be vulnerable with you, and partner with her to find solutions to her problems.

WOMEN, GIRLS, TRANS, NONBINARY FOLK

If you are reading this book, know that you are not alone. No matter what challenges you have faced, others have also faced those challenges. No matter how obscure your special interest, there are others who share your delight in it. No matter how difficult your journey has been and continues to be, there are those ahead of you on that road who can share what works for them.

Do not let anyone make you feel "less than" or unworthy. You are worthy, exactly as you are, without having to earn your place in the world.

It's okay to finally un-mask, to be who you truly are, not who others want you to be. The world needs more you. And you are the only one, the perfect one, for the job.

In Their Own Words

"Learning about autism started my journey of discovery into why I am the way I am. Recently, after sharing my diagnosis with my mother, she asked me what I intended to gain from this knowledge. I thought, 'That's a really good question.' There is no magic pill or cure for autism, nor should there be. Everyone is wired uniquely for themselves, and I am no different! I am not flawed, nor do I have a deficit. I just approach things in my own way.

"I guess what I hope most to gain from my diagnosis is acceptance. Acceptance from myself most all: I don't have to be like everyone else to be included and to be loved. I, in all my glorious and not-so-glorious quirkiness, am deserving of a happy and healthy life!"

— *Shanda K, diagnosed at age 51*

RESOURCES

Adamou, Marios, Maria Johnson, Bronwen Alty. (2018). "Autism Diagnostic Observation Schedule (ADOS) Scores in Males and Females Diagnosed With Autism: A Naturalistic Study." *Advances in Autism* 4, no. 2 (2018): 49–55. https://doi.org/10.1108/aia-01-2018-0003.

Atherton, Gray, Emma Edisbury, Andrea Piovesan, and Liam Cross. "Autism through the Ages: A Mixed Methods Approach to Understanding How Age and Age of Diagnosis Affect Quality of Life." *Journal of Autism and Developmental Disorders*, 2021. https://doi.org/10.1007/s10803-021-05235-x.

Attwood, Tony. *Asperger's and Girls*. Arlington (Texas): Future Horizons, Inc., 2006.

Craft, Samantha. *Everyday Aspergers*. Lancaster (United Kingdom): Your Stories Matter, 2016.

Endow, Judy. *Learning the Hidden Curriculum: The Odyssey of One Autistic Author*. Shawnee (Kansas): AAPC Publishing, 2012.

Endow, Judy. *Paper Words: Discovering and Living With My Autism*. Shawnee, (Kansas): AAPC Publishing, 2009.

Frazier, Thomas W., Stelios Georgiades, Somer L. Bishop, and Antonio Y. Hardan. "Behavioral and Cognitive Characteristics of Females and Males with Autism in the Simons Simplex Collection." *Journal of the American Academy of Child & Adolescent Psychiatry* 53, no. 3 (2014). https://doi.org/10.1016/j.jaac.2013.12.004.

Gotham, K, and Zachary J. Williams. "Measuring Alexithymia in Autistic People." *Spectrum*, 2021. https://doi.org/10.53053/FWEH2679

Grandin, Temple, and Tony Attwood. *Autism and Girls*. Arlington (Texas): Future Horizons, Inc. 2019.

Grandin, Temple, and Tony Attwood. *Different, Not Less: Inspiring Stories of Achievement and Successful Employment from Adults with Autism, Asperger's, and ADHD*. Arlington (Texas): Future Horizons, Inc., 2020.

Grandin, Temple, and Margaret M. Scariano. *Emergence: Labeled Autistic*. New York: Grand Central Publishing, 2005.

Grandin, Temple, and Sean Barron. *Unwritten Rules of Social Relationships: Decoding Social Mysteries Through the Unique Perspectives of Autism*. Arlington (Texas): Future Horizons, Inc., 2017.

Head, Alexandra M, Jane A McGillivray, and Mark A Stokes. "Gender Differences in Emotionality and Sociability in Children with Autism Spectrum Disorders." *Journal of the American Academy of Child & Adolescent Psychiatry* 53, no. 3 (2014): 329–40. https://doi.org/10.1186/2040-2392-5-19.

Hendrickx, Sarah. *Women and Girls with Autism Spectrum Disorder: Understanding Life Experiences from Early Childhood to Old Age*. Philadelphia: Jessica Kingsley Publishers, 2015.

Hornby, Albert Sydney. *Oxford Advanced Learner's Dictionary of Current English*. Edited by Jonathan Crowther. Oxford: Oxford University Press, 1995.

Lee, Jane. "Diagnosis Eludes Many Girls With Autism, Study Says." Spectrum Newsletter, September 3, 2012. https://www.spectrumnews.org/news/diagnosis-eludes-many-girls-with-autism-study-says/.

Lesko, Anita. *Becoming an Autism Success Story*. Arlington (Texas): Future Horizons, Inc., 2019.

Loomes, Rachel, Laura Hull, and William Polmear Mandy. "What Is the Male-to-Female Ratio in Autism Spectrum Disorder? A Systematic Review and

RESOURCES

Meta-Analysis." *Journal of the American Academy of Child & Adolescent Psychiatry* 56, no. 6 (2017): 466–74. https://doi.org/10.1016/j.jaac.2017.03.013.

Maenner, Matthew J., Kelly A. Shaw; Jon Baio, Anita Washington, Mary Patrick, Monica DiRienzo, Deborah L. Christensen, Lisa D. Wiggins, Sydney Pettygrove, Jennifer G. Andrews, et al. "Prevalence and Characteristics of Autism Spectrum Disorder among Children Aged 8 Years—Autism and Developmental Disabilities Monitoring Network, 11 Sites, United States, 2012." *Autism and Developmental Disabilities Monitoring Network* 69, no. SS-4 (2020): 1–12. https://doi.org/10.15585/mmwr.mm6745a7.

Myles, Brenda Smith, Judy Endow, and Malcolm Mayfield. *The Hidden Curriculum of Getting and Keeping a Job: Navigating the Social Landscape of Employment.* Shawnee Mission: AAPC Publishing, 2013.

Oien, Roald. "Asperger's and Girls by Tony Attwood, Temple Grandin, Teresa Bolick, Catherine Faherty, Lisa Iland, Jennifer McIlwee Myers, Ruth Snyder, Sheila Wagner, and Mary Wrobel." *Journal of Autism and Developmental Disorders* 45, no. 1 (2014): 272–72. https://doi.org/10.1007/s10803-014-2209-4.

O'Toole, Jennifer Cook. *Autism in Heels: The Untold Story of a Female Life on the Spectrum.* New York: Skyhorse Publishing, Inc., 2018.

Pecora, Laura A., Grace I. Hancock, Merrilyn Hooley, David H. Demmer, Tony Attwood, Gary B. Mesibov, and Mark A. Stokes. "Gender Identity, Sexual Orientation and Adverse Sexual Experiences in Autistic Females." *Molecular Autism* 11, no. 1 (2020). https://doi.org/10.1186/s13229-020-00363-0.

Purkis, Yenn, and Wenn Lawson. *The Autistic Trans Guide to Life.* London: Jessica Kingsley Publishers, 2021.

Simone, Rudy. *Aspergirls.* London: Jessica Kingsley Publishers, 2010.

Sparrow, Maxfield. Spectrums: *Autistic Transgender People in Their Own Words*. London: Jessica Kingsley Publishers, 2020.

Sturrock, Alexandra, Catherine Adams, and Jenny Freed. "A Subtle Profile with a Significant Impact: Language and Communication Difficulties for Autistic Females without Intellectual Disability." *Frontiers in Psychology* 12 (2021). https://doi.org/10.3389/fpsyg.2021.621742.

Szavalitz, Maia. "Autism—It's Different in Girls." Scientific American, 2016. https://felicity-house.org/wp-content/uploads/2018/02/Autism-Its-Different-in-Girls-Scientific-American-copy-1.pdf.

Willey, Liane Holiday. *Pretending to be Normal: Living with Asperger's Syndrome*. London: Jessica Kingsley Publishers, 1999.

Wright, Jessica. "Clinical Research: Autism Threshold Higher in Girls than Boys: Spectrum: Autism Research News." Spectrum, January 11, 2012. https://www.spectrumnews.org/news/clinical-research-autism-threshold-higher-in-girls-than-boys/.

Wendela Whitcomb Marsh is an award-winning author and autism assessment specialist. In addition to her newest book, *Recognizing Autism in Women and Girls: When It Has Been Hidden Well*, her works include *The ABCs of Autism in the Classroom: Setting the Stage for Success* for educators and *Independent Living with Autism: Your Roadmap to Success* for autistic adults. She co-authored *Homeschooling, Autism Style: Reset for Success* with Siobhan Marsh and *Autism Parent Handbook: Start with the End Goal in Mind* with Dr. Raun Melmed. Those on the spectrum, especially women and others who struggle for recognition, are among her favorite people. Dr. Marsh lives in Salem, Oregon, where she owns PIPS for Autism, LLC: Promoting Independence and Problem Solving. Learn more about her books and speaking at *www.WendelaWhitcombMarsh.com* and about her telehealth autism assessment services at *www.pipsforautism.com*.

Did you like this book?

Rate it and share your opinion!

BARNES&NOBLE
BOOKSELLERS
www.bn.com

amazon.com

Not what you expected? Tell us!

Most negative reviews occur when the book did not reach expectation. Did the description build any expectations that were not met? Let us know how we can do better.

Please drop us a line at info@fhautism.com.
Thank you so much for your support!

FUTURE HORIZONS

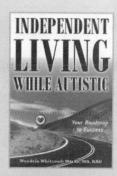

Books by Dr. Temple Grandin

Inspiring Stories of Achievement and Successful Employment from Adults with Autism, Asperger's, and ADHD

Revised and Updated

DIFFERENT NOT LESS

DR. TEMPLE GRANDIN

Foreword by Tony Attwood, PhD

AUTISM & EDUCATION

THE WAY 🍎 I SEE IT

DR. TEMPLE GRANDIN

What Parents and Teachers Need to Know

Updated & Revised Fifth Edition

DR. TEMPLE GRANDIN

THE WAY I SEE IT

A Personal Look at Autism

Foreword by Tony Attwood, PhD

82 SUBJECT. COVERED

TEMPLE Grandin

The STORIES I Tell My FRIENDS

by Anita Lesko — Foreword by Mick Jackson
Emmy Award-winning director of
the HBO Movie Temple Grandin

UNWRITTEN RULES

Dr. Temple Grandin & Sean Barron

OF SOCIAL RELATIONSHIPS

New Edition with Author Updates

Decoding Social Mysteries Through Autism's Unique Perspectives

edited by Veronica Zysk

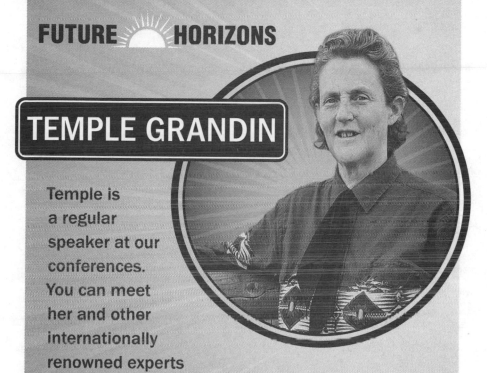